No Hurdle Too High

No Hurdle Too High

The Story of Show Jumper Margie Goldstein Engle

by Mona Pastroff Goldstein
Foreword by Margie Goldstein Engle

THE LYONS PRESS
Guilford, Connecticut

An imprint of The Globe Pequot Press

The Lyons Press is an imprint of The Globe Pequot Press.

10 9 8 7 6 5 4 3 2 1

Printed in the United States of America

Designed by Carol Sawyer, Rose Design

ISBN 1-59228-683-6

Library of Congress Cataloging-in-Publication Data

Goldstein, Mona Pastroff.
  No hurdle too high : the story of show jumper Margie Goldstein Engle / Mona Pastroff Goldstein.
    p. cm.
  Includes bibliographical references.
  ISBN 1-59228-683-6 (trade cloth)
  1. Goldstein-Engle, Margie. 2. Show jumpers (Persons)--Florida--Biography. 3. Show jumping--United States. I. Title.
SF295.535.G65G65 2005
798.2'5'092--dc22
                                                    2005021582

To people everywhere who pursue their dreams.

The future belongs to those who believe in the beauty of their dreams.

Eleanor Roosevelt

No throne can compare with the back of a horse, and there is no way in which man can come closer to nature than by becoming one with a horse.

William Steinkraus

Contents

Contents

Foreword

My career wasn't built just by horses, but by people as well. I would love to acknowledge them all if I could, but that would be another book. Most of them know who they are (such as Bibby Farmer, Penny Fires, Karen Harndon Smith, Jan Frances, Patti Harnois, and "Spank" Deemer). I thank them all.

Certainly there were some very special people in my life. Robert and Dorothy Kramer opened their hearts and their home to me when I was nine. I will never forget their generosity and their loyalty. They were the best people with whom I could have started my journey into the world of horses.

A very special thanks to my parents who, even though they thought I was crazy, supported me every step of the way. They were always there when I needed them the most. The attributes they possess—integrity, high moral standards, a good work ethic, and a great sense of humor—are my guidelines. They have come a long way in their understanding of an industry that was totally alien to them. It is a joy to see them every Sunday during Florida's Winter Fair rooting me on. I will never be able to thank them enough.

I have been especially blessed with great owners. They put their trust in me, and in return I gave them every ounce of determination that was within me. I consider myself fortunate that many of my owners also became my friends. As friends we have shared much, and in doing so we have had great fun.

I know firsthand how much the industry owes to the sponsors. For example, Budweiser has not just supported the Grand Prix circuit, but also been wonderful to me on a personal level.

The horses you will read about in this book are just a few of those who took me where I wanted to go (and sometimes where I didn't want to go).

I feel fortunate and blessed that these great horses and people have come into my life. I fell in love with these animals when I was nine, and that love continues to grow even now.

In this business, anyone would have a difficult time getting anything accomplished without great help. I would like to thank all the grooms and exercise riders who have been with me over the years. Many thanks, also, to all the veterinarians who have cared for the health and the well-being of the many horses under my charge. They have dedicated their lives to the care of the horse. Without them, I could not have accomplished the monumental task that I set out to do.

I would also like to express my gratitude and love to my husband, Steve, who has helped me every step of the way. I thank him for his patience and understanding with our hectic and crazy lifestyle. I thank him for taking care of me and especially my horses. In reading this book I hope that everyone gets the take-home message that with hard work, determination, and great people, your dreams can come true.

Margie Goldstein Engle

Acknowledgments

For their patience and guidance, I would like to thank and acknowledge the South Florida Writers Association. The critique group, of which I was a member, offered me helpful and insightful suggestions.

My education was further enhanced when two giants in the field of show jumping, George Morris and William Steinkraus, encouraged and directed my efforts to Elizabeth Carnes, the publisher-owner of Half Halt Press, Incorporated. Beth not only read the manuscript but also sent it to freelance writer Kimberly Gatto for review. Kim, the author of *Michelle Kwan: Champion on Ice* and *An Apple a Day*, is also an accomplished equestrienne. Her knowledgeable suggestions to me, a nonrider, made me aware of the unique features and required preparation of the sport. She continues to be extremely supportive and helpful.

Without my family, there would be no book. They provided the events, of course. But more than that, each offered direct assistance. My husband, Irv, can spot a misspelled word or a run-on sentence from twenty feet away. Surely he could have made a career as a proofreader if needed. Margie provided me with time, of which she has little, and background, of which she has much. Her husband, Steve, and my grandson Jeff served admirably as computer consultants. My older grandson Matthew, an accomplished fiction writer, reviewed and critiqued the results.

This updated and expanded *No Hurdle Too High* would never have been possible were it not for the support of two amazing people. My agent, Kim Tudor, had the foresight and belief in Margie's story to bring it to the attention of The Lyons Press. Throughout the preparation of the book, Kim continued with her unique assistance. My editor, Steven D. Price, provided encouragement, knowledge, and an unlimited supply of patience and understanding. It has been a privilege to work with them both.

Acknowledgments

To the photographers who captured the beauty and strength of this dangerous sport, I honor and respect the integrity you bring to your task. To one and all, I offer thanks and appreciation.

M. P. G.

CHAPTER ONE

Introduction to the World of Show Jumping

EVERY SUNDAY AFTERNOON FOR THE FIRST TWO MONTHS OF THE YEAR, we left our home in Miami, pointed our car north, and drove to the Palm Beach Equestrian Shows.

"Hurry, Irv, hurry. We'll miss the riders walking the course."

"Easy does it, Mona. Let's see if we have everything."

My methodical husband could not be rushed. He looked around the car. "Okay, we have our sunglasses, our hats. We'll get the programs at the gate. I'll put these papers for Margie in the trunk until after the show."

I shifted from one foot to the other. On this crisp, cool afternoon in February 1997, the sun's soothing rays almost succeeded in banishing the anxiety I always felt before one of our daughter's horse shows.

We headed toward the opening of the Palm Beach Equestrian Center, maneuvering our way through hordes of children, adults, and an assortment of Jack Russell terriers, dachshunds, and other well-cared-for dogs. "They sure do love their animals," I said to Irv. "It looks as much like a dog show as a horse one."

The voices of several announcers from different areas blurred together as we walked toward the international arena. The smells of grilling meats, soft pretzels, and pungent fruits floated on the gentle breeze. We walked around the vivid yellow-and-white-striped tents and worked our way to the west-side bleachers, anticipating and hoping to avoid the intensity of the later sun.

"Mrs. Goldstein, Mr. Goldstein, over here, over here." We looked around to see where the voice was calling from and spotted Nancy Unger, Margie's friend, pointing to the seats she had saved for us. Most of the spectators were already seated, but some stood in friendly clusters, chatting excitedly about the equestrian show-jumping event awaiting us.

"I'm so proud of Margie," said Nancy. "Here we are at the largest and most important Grand Prix in the country this year, and Marge is going to break records today."

I reached out and hugged my daughter's loyal friend "Please, God, let that be the *only* thing she breaks! Oh, Nancy, let's talk about something—*anything*—else. Doesn't the field look beautiful?"

The spacious emerald-green arena glowed with potted plants and flowers next to colorful hurdles, carefully designed to please the crowd and distract the horses. The multihued sponsors' emblems vied with the bright yellow, red, orange, and purple bouquets that accented most of the jumps. Bushy olive-colored raffia palms waved gently by the sides of the wide black-and-white-striped oxers. By the SeaWorld obstacle, plastic dolphins stood ready to leap. The bleachers in front of the airy tents bustled with activity from the excited fans, anxious to watch the final 1996 American Grand Prix (AGA) competition and see the presentation of the AGA Rider of the Year Award.

Irv spied Karen Harndon, Margie's childhood riding instructor, and called out, "Hey, Karen, come join us."

"From the looks of things, I got here just in time. I see they must have posted the course design."

Men and women in red or black jackets streamed into the arena. The riders strode purposefully: walking the field, checking out the fences, noting the distance between them, and mentally converting their own steps to the number of horse strides needed to position their steeds for each liftoff. This walk-through introduced the rider to the day's specific course. Their horses would see it for the first time when the class began.

"Which one is Margie?" asked one of Nancy's riding pupils.

"Look for the smallest one," Nancy replied. She then turned to me. "Remember when the professionals told her she'd never make it in the world of show jumping? They said she was much too little to control all that brute power."

"I remember they wanted her to be a jockey, but you know our gal. The more they told her she couldn't reach Grand Prix level, the more determined she became."

We quickly located Margie's petite form, watched her pace off the strides, and laughed as she stretched her legs as far as they would extend.

I turned to my husband and said, "Do you realize what those thirty riders out there represent? Many of them are her childhood heroes. There are Olympians with gold and silver medals, World Cup contenders, Nation's Cup winners—that's quite a group!"

Irv responded, "Well, Mona, Margie's the only one out there who has ever been Rider of the Year four times. You don't have to worry about her credentials."

"It's her *body* I worry about. I'll be glad when this is over and she's safe!" We were in for a long wait. Margie and the other twenty-nine American participants had earned their standings after a year of intense competition. They would ride in reverse order, and because of her high ranking, she was scheduled to ride next to last. The winner of the previous year's class, Laura Chapot, would ride last.

When the competition began, we watched each horse-and-rider combination. They were beautiful to observe—strong, graceful, and skilled. But the course designer from Bolivia, Jose "Pepe" Gamarra, had done his job too well, judging by what followed. Pepe, knowing that he was dealing with top riders and scopey horses, those with natural athletic ability, filled the large field with difficult obstacles. To complete the thirteen numbered jumps, sixteen jumping efforts, the riders would have to make many sharp turns to stay within the time limit of ninety-two seconds. Particularly challenging were both the number eight triple combination and the number twelve double combination. Also, the space between the two fences of each oxer measured more than five feet, so that the horses would have to not only clear the heights but also stretch out to clear the widths. There was nothing easy on this field! Every rail knocked down at any obstacle,

3

and every hoof in the water or on the tape of the water jump, would add four faults to a rider's score.

The talented Anne Kursinski, who had recently won the team silver medal from the 1996 Olympics as well as medals in two previous Olympics, rode third. The tricky space within the triple caused her horse, Suddenly, to knock down the top rails on both the 8a and 8b fences for a total of eight penalty faults. The efforts continued. No one rode fault-free. At midway in the competition, two riders had four faults, which placed them in the lead.

Fellow 1996 Olympic winner Peter Leone galloped onto the field. His strong, solid showing through the triple thrilled the spectators. Just as he rode from 12a to 12b, though, Crown Royal Let's Go took a small half stride before jumping the second half of the combination. His hoof hit the fence, and it thudded to the ground.

Next McLain Ward, the 1991 Rookie of the Year, took the field atop Orchestre. The breathless announcer cheered the first clear round, but added, "Two seconds over the time allowed. There will be a half-point time fault." McLain was now out in front.

The thrilling duo of Michael Matz and Rhum IV entered the fray, and the spectators roared in anticipation. Michael had not only won the 1996 team silver for the United States in Atlanta but also had been selected to lead the entire U.S. Olympic delegation and carry our flag for the final victory parade. This unassuming hero, who had risked his life when he rescued passengers from an airline crash only a few years earlier, rode beautifully. Rhum's hoof hit the last fence of the triple. It rocked in the cup, but it did not fall. They approached the number ten hurdle, painted to blend easily with the earth below. Rhum hit the top rail with his front legs, and the sound of its falling seemed to echo throughout the arena. Michael joined the group of eight riders with four faults.

Margie and Hidden Creek's Laurel, a beautiful dark bay (brown), Dutch-bred mare, entered the ring. While the loudspeaker introduced them, they walked slowly past the most colorful and distracting hurdles. This effort to show eight-year-old Laurel the obstacles was Margie's deliberate way of reassuring her. "See, Laurel? There's nothing here that we can't navigate. We'll do it together."

They cantered slowly, then picked up speed as the buzzer signaled them to begin. When Laurel passed through the sensors, the time clock was set in motion. Margie banished all thoughts except the strides to count, the placement of Laurel's legs just before takeoff, the time to save with tighter turns. Each lift began with Margie squeezing her calf and lower leg around Laurel; each landing prompted her calculation to position the horse in the proper direction for the next jump.

They jumped the first hurdle, an oxer, and Laurel's rear leg nicked a rail lightly. The fence rattled, but stayed upright. "Settle down, Laurel. We need to clear these hurdles with ease." Margie focused these thoughts toward the mare at the same time she pulled the reins with her left hand and pressed her right leg in the same direction. When Laurel responded quickly, Margie now felt safe to press her faster and tighten the turns.

"Okay, girl. We need to pay attention to the rails on top of the water hazard." Margie balanced Laurel's front end with the reins so the horse would not be spooked by the glare from the water beneath them. She squeezed her calves together to signal Laurel across the oxer. She heard the cheers of the crowd, but blocked out all thoughts except the next fence.

As they approached the Budweiser fence with the six-foot bottles on the sides and the rails in shallow cups, Margie eased Laurel upward, adjusting her body so they could avoid even a breeze to interfere with the lightly balanced obstacle. This fence had fallen for several competitors, and the two athletes—horse and rider—were taking no chances. The successful high jump prompted applause as Margie turned her mare sharply. "Good girl," Margie thought, "that ought to save us a fraction of a second!"

Next came the oxer whose fences stretched across five feet, six inches in width. Laurel and Margie were now responding as one, so that the push of Margie's heels propelled the horse strongly forward. They galloped quickly toward the treacherous triple. One stride, two, jump. One stride, jump. One stride, two, jump. They sailed over the camouflaged number ten and across the last line of four jumps in rapid succession. The spectators were on their feet. As Margie and Laurel raced toward the last fence, the murmur erupted into a roar. "Careful, Laurel. We don't want to lose the class at the last hurdle." They soared over the final obstacle as the announcer screamed over the noise of the crowd: "The first clean round!

HORSE INTERNATIONAL

SPORT & BREEDING

With the Official News of the FEI, the IJRC, the IDRC, the IERA and the WBFSH

& ACHTENBACH

1997   *Horse International* recognized Margie and Hidden Creek's Laurel, shown above winning Budweiser's American Grand Prix Association (AGA) Championship Grand Prix event. U.S. correspondent Nancy Jaffer reported that Margie won the award for three years in a row: 1994, 1995, and 1996, as well as in 1989 and 1991. The article noted that it was the first time in AGA's twenty-two-year history that one owner (Michael Polaski of Hidden Creek Farms) had taken both prizes for the year. Alvaretto won Horse of the Year; Laurel became Reserve Champion. Also, it was the first time one rider had so completely dominated the standings. Even in the final AGA Championship Grand Prix, there was no jump-off. Margie had the only clear round.
Photographer: *Bob Langrish*

Ladies and gentlemen, there will be no jump-off unless Laura also has a clear round. Margie Goldstein Engle—the first four-time winner is now the first *five*-time AGA Rider of the Year!"

As Margie and Laurel took their tame victory lap around the arena followed by McLain and then Laura, her father and I eased our way toward the opening where her fans had already assembled. My husband reminisced, "Remember when Margie first asked if she could take lessons?"

"I remember being so worried I told her she could only walk, trot, and canter; that *jumping* the hurdles was much too dangerous. Who knew her childhood hobby would lead to *this*?"

The memories flooded back.

CHAPTER TWO

Enter Smiling

HAPPINESS. GRATITUDE. DELIGHT. Is it possible that the birth of one small baby could generate so many joyful and fulfilling emotions? Even the little house in West Miami where we Goldsteins lived seemed to glow with the excitement of Margie's arrival.

The year was 1958. At that time my husband Irvin was a CPA and I was a full-time wife and mother. The family included our sons, Mark, who was then eight and a half years old, and Eddie, who was almost seven. A little over a year prior, we had lost a baby girl, and the empty spots in our hearts loomed large. When Margie was born on March 31 of that year, our joy knew no bounds. Mark and Eddie simply adored their baby sister and wanted to spoil her—if only Irv and I would let them.

However, when she began to walk, chancing upon their prized belongings, the results were not always appreciated. "Mark, did you spill my marbles all over the closet?"

"No, Eddie. Did you take my Invisible Man apart?"

Even closing the door to their room didn't prevent the inquisitive little girl from her explorations. "Mom, she's mixed all the puzzle pieces into one big heap!"

Somehow her mischievous smile, sparkling brown eyes, and appreciation of their every action would win them over once again. "Mom, Margie is going to be one year old today. Who did you invite for her birthday?"

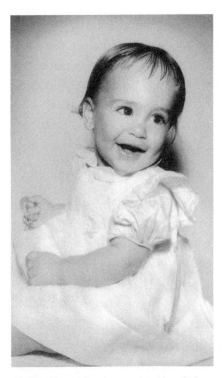

1959 When Margie reached her first-year birthday, brothers Mark and Eddie made sure there was a celebration.

"The family is coming over Sunday for a celebration."

"No *children* for our Margie?"

"How could you forget?"

I went about my business until suddenly Mark and Eddie led a group of children to the front door. "Mom, these are Margie's friends. Now we can have a *real* birthday party."

Her brothers had corrected their mother's "error." Quickly, I searched the pantry to find drinks and sweets for this eager-to-celebrate crew.

The Goldstein offspring really enjoyed this pattern of two birthday parties per year—one for the family, one for each child's friends. However, Margie needed a little explanation one year. "Honey, have you put away all your toys? The family will be here tonight to celebrate your birthday."

My daughter looked perplexed. "Celebrate my birthday? I don't understand."

"What don't you understand?"

"We just *had* a birthday party and I was three. Now the family is coming over for *another* birthday party. Am I four?" Her brothers assured her everything was fine and she was not aging too rapidly!

Margie loved playing with her older brothers, and she longed to join them in their baseball and football games. "Mark, Eddie, I want to play with you, too. May I be on your team?"

"Margie, you don't know how. You can't pitch. You can't catch. You're too little. Why don't you play with someone else, someone your own age?"

Perhaps this is why Margie learned persistence at such an early age. The more they told her she wasn't good enough, the more she practiced. Day after day, she would throw a ball into a tire, patiently performing this task over and over until her control over the ball became more and more apparent. Still her big brothers remained unconvinced.

Four-year-old Margie sought the solace of a wonderful imaginary friend. "Okay, if you won't play with me, Teekie will!" Teekie was a little girl mouse who very much wanted to be a boy mouse, and she never, ever said no when Margie wanted to play ball.

Irv and I watched Mark's and Eddie's reactions with great curiosity, never sure whether they were embarrassed that their younger sister talked to someone they couldn't see or if they appreciated her daily ball practice. One afternoon, Margie's determination paid off. Mark and Eddie prepared for a quick game of backyard baseball, but there were too few boys who could be rounded up at the last minute.

"Margie, now's your chance. Let's see what you can do."

No second invitation was needed. Little and young as she was, she could pitch and catch as well as any of the neighborhood gang. What she lacked in stature and experience, she more than made up for in determination and willingness to extend her efforts toward the required practice. From then on, Mark and Eddie made sure their little sister *always* played on their team. A few years later, when she became captain and pitcher of her elementary school's softball team, her brothers expressed little surprise. Of course; hadn't they "trained" her well?

CHAPTER THREE

Home Is Where the Animals Are

THE LACK OF ROOM IN OUR SMALL WEST MIAMI HOUSE sent us looking for larger quarters. My brother Eddie and his recent bride, Nancy, lived on a beautiful, secluded little lake that we thought would be ideal for our growing family. We built a home large enough for the five of us and one that each of us would appreciate for different reasons.

Irv and I loved the refuge of a quiet country life in the midst of a bustling city. Our front yard faced a narrow stretch of road only four blocks long, so we had little traffic to disturb us. The view from our family room and kitchen at the back of the house overlooked the calm water and included a little beach we had built on the shore. We anticipated entertaining family and friends in this relaxed atmosphere, and I planted small trees in the backyard to shade us from the reflected glare of the setting sun. "Please, grow, grow," I would say to them as I carefully fertilized, watered, and sprayed.

Our home provided storage space and living space. Even our dachshund, Count Edmark Von Uberheim, found a place to hide when Margie's attention overwhelmed him. Most of the time, he was very patient when she gave him her full attention. She loved to dress him in the family castoffs, and he would stand—still but stylish. Our little clothes designer would pick him up and bring him over for me to admire. "Mommy, isn't he beautiful?" Count was very happy when he could escape.

11

Margie regarded Sunrise Lake as her own private nature preserve, and we quickly realized how much our preschool daughter loved animals. Fortunately, the strange creatures that our little boys found so appealing were familiar, not frightening, objects. I was quite used to either Mark or Eddie saying, "Mommy, hold out your hand and close your eyes. I brought you a present." After complying with the request, I would open my eyes to see my reward: a squashed bug, a squiggling worm, or a retreating-into-its-shell snail.

However, Margie brought that fascination to a new high. Jars disappeared only to reappear filled with tadpoles, small fish, or unidentified green slime. Wild birds waited for their nightly bread crumbs. Even lizards didn't escape the watchful eye of the family zookeeper. She made little leashes for them and happily walked them from one end of the patio to the other.

Our daughter also enjoyed playing with the little girls who lived next door, Denise and Kelly. They had a multitude of animals, including a mischievous little coatimundi, which is a creature that looks half monkey, half raccoon. This impish animal would jump to the top shelf and proceed to knock down bottles, jars—anything that would make a loud crashing noise—much to the delight of the audience below. "That's funny," Margie giggled as her two friends joined in the laughter.

"You girls think that's so funny?" replied Denise and Kelly's mother. "Then you can help me clean up."

One day, the girls found four abandoned kittens who could not have been more than one or two days old. Something bad must have happened to their mother, because they were so young and helpless. Margie had little trouble convincing us that she could care for them. And care for them she did. Every few hours, Margie and I fed the kittens with a doll bottle. When they still mewed pitifully, she wiped them carefully with a damp rag much as a mother cat might lick them.

"How did you know to do that?" I asked with some surprise.

"I watched," came the matter-of-fact reply.

The tiny animals thrived, and Margie—as instructed—found homes for all except one small yellow tabby whom she was allowed to keep.

Frisky was a most unusual cat. He didn't know he wasn't supposed to like water, so he followed Margie everywhere—even right into the lake when she went swimming. As she splashed happily in the gentle water, he eagerly and furiously cat-paddled right by her side. Nor did he know he wasn't a human. When family members returned to his home, he greeted them by jumping into their arms, placing his paws around their necks, and licking their cheeks.

When Margie turned six and was old enough to go to school, her interest in animals continued. "Honey, what are you doing?" I asked one day.

"I'm working on a science project, Mom. May I use the old lamp?"

When Margie attended South Miami Elementary School where I taught, she often waited in my classroom so we could ride home together. The work of the older children fascinated her, and she longed to be a fourth-grader and do all those "neat things."

I examined what Margie had put together so far and nodded in approval. "Honey, you've built yourself quite an incubator, but where did you get those eggs?"

She explained that she had followed a female duck to her nest and "borrowed" a few of the contents. I smiled. The possibility was far greater that our would-be scientist would hard-boil rather than hatch the eggs.

A few weeks later, an excited voice boomed out, "Mom, Dad, come quickly. The eggs are hatching!"

Yes, there did seem to be a few cracks, but—of course—our doting daughter could have done that when she turned them over each day. We watched for a while and then went about our routine.

The evening stretched from one lengthy minute to another. Our foster "mommy" kept a close watch on her "babies," but by eight o'clock she reluctantly headed for her bed.

The next morning, we woke to unfamiliar sounds coming from the patio. When we went to investigate, we saw our delighted daughter with a happy grin on her face and three fluffy little yellow ducklings peeping contentedly in her arms.

The next few weeks were very exciting ones for our daughter. Wherever she led, the little ducklings followed. A swim in the lake resulted in first Margie, then one–two–three balls of yellow fluff behind her. When she played football with her friends, her ducklings learned to scamper—

1963   When Margie was in kinder-
garten, she met her first pony.

Frisky followed Margie everywhere—
even swimming into our lake.

1963   Margie, Mona, Irvin, Mark, and Eddie Goldstein sat for a family picture
minus animals.

fast! And when she simply walked from one place to another, the ducks walked all in a line behind her. Our neighbors smiled when they saw the feathered new residents. After all, it wasn't every lake that could boast of a parade that consisted of one small girl, followed by her own Huey, Dewey, and Louie.

Whether they waddled on two feet or walked on four, it was a definite advantage to be an animal in Margie's world. How much of an advantage, we would one day find out.

CHAPTER FOUR

Love and Friendships

SCHOOL FOR MARGIE WAS A CONSTANT SOURCE OF PLEASURE—more friends to enjoy and more adventures to seek! Weekend sleepovers, although mis-named, became wonderful events to be shared among her pals. The Ping-Pong table was folded and moved to another room. The piano was nestled out of the way in one of the living room corners. The girls set up their sleeping bags, pillows, and stuffed animals on the padded carpeted area and settled in for the night.

Many hours would pass before they finally closed their eyes. Pillow fights were a requirement. Then they called for Margie's guitar ballads. Her songs touted the high jinks of each girl present, followed by much strumming, which gave her time to think about her next chorus. She was no Bonnie Raitt, but her friends thought she was the greatest lyricist they knew. And of course, each evening had its own variations: scary stories followed by nervous laughter; silly jokes and funny faces accompanied by prolonged shrieks.

When horses became part of their world, their activities expanded to include jumping over imaginary hurdles, cantering, and whinnying.

"Is that Margie telling *another* joke?" We would lie in our bed, trying unsuccessfully to fall asleep. "Nancy hasn't stopped giggling since they've gone to bed!" "What on earth are Sherri and Bobbi doing? It sounds as if they're conducting a séance!" The entertainment always ended in the same way—with Margie's dad roaring, "Okay, girls, that's enough! Quiet!" Another successful sleepover!

One weekend, when Margie had slept overnight at her friend Andrea Marks's house, they spent the following day at Gladewinds Farm. Between second and third grades, Andrea had gone to summer camp, which included horseback riding at this stable. That one day was all it took. Our delighted daughter was completely captivated!

From the moment Margie met the horses, she dreamed and talked of little else. The Kramers, who owned the farm, were confronted with a determined nine-year-old who would do any job around the barn or the dog and cat kennels just to be near the horses. For six months, she would come home from Gladewinds and tell her family, "They *let* me muck out the barn. They *let* me curry the horses."

We looked at one another in amazement. "Margie, what are you talking about? Exactly what do you do out there?"

"Well, the stalls have to be clean. If the horses stand in their own waste, they may get sick. So I muck—shovel out the manure and wet spots—and bring in fresh hay and their feed. And of course, their coats have to be clean also, so I use a curry comb and brush them with hard and soft brushes until they shine. Oh, Mom, Dad, you should see Holly. When I finish brushing her, she rubs her nose against my shoulder. And Garnet . . ."

"Yes, Margie, we get the idea. If you're willing to do what you just described, we'll work something out."

After Irv and I discussed it, we struck a bargain with our daughter. "Honey, if you're willing to keep up your good work at home and school—chores and homework—we'll pay for once-a-week lessons."

For me, it was like visiting a new world without a map or guide of any kind. I had never been on a horse or pony, never visited a farm.

As we drove toward Gladewinds, my white-knuckled hands gripped the steering wheel. Margie had trouble keeping still as we headed toward her long-awaited first lesson. I dropped off my bouncing, wide-eyed daughter, and while she ran to the designated instructional area, I parked quickly and rushed to catch up with her. "Margie, wait. Here's your ticket." I held a small packet of fifteen coupons and handed her the first one.

The fenced-in arena was bare, but the nearby trees rustled with a gentle breeze and shaded the children and ponies from the afternoon sun. Margie was helped onto a small gray pony named Sandpiper and joined three other girls and one young boy, who each sat astride what to me looked like a toy-sized horse.

The instructor, JoAnn Buress, explained the goals for the day, ". . . and the most important thing you'll learn is how to *post,* how to get in rhythm with the horse's trot. When he steps forward with his outside leg, you'll step out of the saddle and up on your stirrup. As his leg moves back, you'll sit back down. Up and down, feel the rhythm. Now, walk. Now, trot. Cluck—make a clucking sound. Children, squeeze your legs together as I showed you—sounds, signals—you're letting your horse know what you want."

Five little ponies alternately walked or trotted. I couldn't tell whether they were listening to the teacher's voice or following the children's signals, but as the lesson progressed, I began to relax. The competence of the instructor was obvious, and the behavior of the eager children and gentle ponies reflected their total involvement.

The hour passed quickly. "Mom, Mom, did you see? Did you see?"

"I did. Margie, you were great!"

The instructor joined us. "Are you sure your daughter has never had lessons before? I've never seen anyone pick up posting so quickly."

Margie exploded into the conversation. "I've been watching when you teach the children."

"*You're* the eager one!"

And that eagerness never left. The next week, the children were introduced to picking up cantering and correct leads. When she wasn't at a lesson, Margie was on the phone with Andrea or Bobbi or Sherri discussing what they were learning and what they just "luh-uh-ved" about each pony and horse. "And I pressed my left leg into his side, and he made a right lead—just like he was supposed to. Oh, it's such fun!"

"Can you ride your horse smoothly when you walk or trot? Are you able to make Sweet Charity pick up the canter right from the walk without trotting?"

The phone lines vibrated with their excitement.

"Margie," I said one day, "I'm so glad you're enjoying your riding. We have some worries, though. I heard some of the parents talk about a child at another barn who fell when she was jumping. She's paralyzed from the neck down. We'll let you take lessons and practice on the flat ground. You can walk, trot, or canter, but no jumping. It's just too dangerous."

"But, Mom—"

"No, honey. We want to keep you in one piece, please, with all the parts moving correctly."

That simple goal was not to be. "Margie, why are you holding your arm so strangely?"

"It's fine. Really it is."

After several days, Irv and I agreed we could wait no longer.

The doctor's words chilled me. "There's an impacted fracture right where the arm joins the shoulder. If you had waited any longer, growth patterns would have been affected. One arm would be shorter than the other."

He immobilized Margie's arm, tying it to her body. "I'll see you in three weeks. Meanwhile, you will not move that arm at all. How did you do this?"

Margie looked at me pleadingly. "It wasn't the horse's fault. I was riding bareback, standing up. It's *my* fault. I was goofing around." This became her pattern. Never could her steed do any wrong. *She* must have been in error.

Her father and I, striving for balance between worry for her physical safety and pride in all the positive character development we noted, spoke to her that evening. "You've got to realize how serious this could be. Margie, you must use common sense around the horses or the lessons stop."

Although Margie said all the right words, years later we would learn how many chances she took. She and her friends continued riding bareback, standing, or riding two at a time. When we finally heard about those foolhardy days, Margie responded, "But I was learning to *fall*. I was never afraid to fall, because I knew how to land on my feet."

Still, if it wasn't one problem, it was another. From time to time, I'd have a faculty meeting or a parent conference, and our departure for Gladewinds would be considerably delayed. Margie became extremely enterprising in checking my schedule and arranging carpools that fit our needs.

"Mom, I met a girl at Gladewinds today. I asked her address and she doesn't live too far from us. She said her mother could drive on Wednesdays."

All I needed to do was to point the car in the right direction. Miss Determination had the names, addresses, and days all worked out. When she was older and no car was available, Margie found a bus that let her out one mile from the stable. The two-mile walk to Gladewinds and back was undertaken with no complaints.

One Saturday, when I was carpooling my group of ten-year-olds to Gladewinds, I asked, "What do you all *do* for a whole long day?" Four excited voices rang out.

"I should have known better! Let's start in alphabetical order. You first, Andrea."

"Like today—it's Holly's birthday—we have parties for every one of the ponies on their special day. We make a cake out of molasses, oats, and sugar, with carrots for candles. We—horses, ponies, us—wear our party hats and play games while riding. We have horseless horse shows, too, on foot—and we jump and everything."

My antenna went up. "What kind of games are played while you're on the horses and ponies?"

Margie broke in, "Oh, we have relay races. We'll hold the reins with one hand and with the other hand balance an egg on a spoon, passing it on to the next person."

What she didn't tell me is that at various points in the relay, they jumped on and off the ponies with probably more concern for the egg and spoon than for their own safety. Andrea quickly took back her turn: "We vary the relay games. Sometimes we bob for apples, and sometimes we pop balloons."

"Where do you get all these ideas?"

"Well, those are some of the fun riding classes they have at the gymkhana shows. But we work with our ponies and horses, too. Margie is helping me correct some of Sweet Charity's problems."

Diane added, "And mine, too. Sometimes Gumon can be a brat and not do what I want. He'll get spooked, take off, and then I'm scared. Margie says he's just testing me, so she'll ride him and correct him."

"You know what I like best?" asked Margie, not waiting for a reply. "When we put a dollar or a coin between our legs and the horse's body and see who can ride the longest without the money falling."

I loved listening to Margie and her friends. Watching children grow up so happy, so filled with purpose, so helpful with one another, rejoicing in their own and their friends' accomplishments—I hoped their world could stay like this forever.

When we arrived at the barn, that thought came crashing down as the teacher said to me, "Margie is ready for jumping. You've told me how you feel, but she's so talented. Would you want to hold back children in your class because of parents' unwarranted concerns?"

"Worrying about her physical safety is a whole different matter!"

"Do me a favor. Watch our next group of hunter jumpers. We use crossbars that are high only on one side, low on the other. Where they cross is only one foot high. Gladewinds is one of the most safety-conscious barns in the country. We actually are as concerned for keeping Margie in one piece as you are!"

We—Margie, her dad, and I—spent the whole next week debating this important step. Finally, "Irv, everything I've ever seen out there tells me there couldn't be a better environment for a growing child. They're learning so much more than riding."

He still looked skeptical, so I continued, "I've never seen such compassionate children, such responsible behavior, and I honestly believe all of them—adults, children, animals—understand and read one another's minds. It's just an amazingly happy place."

"Maybe we are being overprotective. Margie, you're such a daredevil. If we agree, will you respect and understand our concerns?"

With Margie's assurances, we reluctantly gave our consent.

As her skill increased, so did her desire for more lessons. "Mom, Dad, Mrs. Kramer told me how good I was getting. I'd be even *better* with more lessons."

"Margie, it cost quite a bit to send Mark to the University of Pennsylvania, and next year, Eddie will be ready to go to college. We simply can't afford it. Additional lessons are not in our budget."

Our little girl did not let a little obstacle like this deter her. She pleaded her case at home and at the barn. "I'm already doing chores at home and babysitting in the neighborhood. Isn't there anything else I can do to earn extra rides and lessons?"

Mrs. Kramer came to the rescue. "Okay, Margie," she responded one day. "You're doing a great job grooming and feeding the horses. You sure aren't afraid of getting dirty when you're cleaning out the barn. Let's see how you work with the cats and dogs in the pet kennel."

Mr. and Mrs. Kramer were impressed and let her work in exchange for her additional lessons from Karen Harndon and Penny Fires. Karen and Penny were in their early twenties, full of vim, vigor, and integrity. Margie looked up to them as expert professionals who had gained great experience when they traveled the Grand Prix circuit. Karen had been a contender for the Olympics and, noting the same ability and willingness in Margie, encouraged her toward a similar goal.

"How's it going, honey?" we would inquire frequently. As a couple of years passed, we realized how wide her knowledge had become.

"Oh, it's just so much fun! Besides my friends asking me to ride their horses, some of the local trainers are asking me also."

"They trust an eleven-year-old?"

"Well, my friends tell me they appreciate my working out problems their horses develop. The Kramers say that the horses sell for more money when they prove they can follow directions. The trainers—Bibby Farmer is one—like that I'm capable and *small*, which helps with the ponies. And of course, I'm already riding and breaking in new ones who were bred at the barn for the beginning students."

"Goodness, you must be riding a great many horses!"

Margie tried to be patient with my complete lack of information about her world. "Not really. Gladewinds has seventy stalls, and at least twenty of them are filled with boarders. As the others improve and are easy to handle, someone always buys them. Then we start all over again."

"Does that mean that you're riding *fifty* horses at any given time?"

Margie laughed. "Oh, Mom! I do different things at different times. When they're about two to three years old, I break them to the saddle and bridle. When they reach four to five, we start them on jumps—but only small ones."

Margie loved riding *all* the mounts—the more difficult the horse, the greater the challenge. Mrs. Kramer teased her, "Margie, you would ride a donkey if we had one!"

As they spent additional time together, the bond between the Kramers and Margie became even stronger. Dorothy Kramer was a patient, gentle lady who thoroughly enjoyed all the children who came to the barn. Mr. Kramer hid his loving nature behind a gruff exterior that frightened some of the young people until they got to know him better. They liked Margie's impish good humor and her proven responsibility, but even as their "fourth daughter," they sometimes despaired at her mischief.

Mrs. Kramer corrected her gently: "Margie, the sprinklers went on right in the middle of Karen's lessons. How do you think that happened?"

Karen threw up her hands and reminded her young pupil, "Will the Mouseketeer please take the underwear off her head? Her two ponytails sticking out of each leg hole don't look the least bit like mouse ears to me. Besides, enough of the singing already!"

Sometimes she simply answered Margie in resigned tones, "Okay, 'Knock, knock. Who's there?' And this is the last joke for today!"

For the most part, they put up with her pranks and jokes, because the work always was done. However, Mrs. Kramer had the last laugh when Margie couldn't find March Lad to school (practice or warm up).

"Mrs. Kramer, Mrs. Kramer, I can't find March Lad! You didn't sell him, did you?"

"No. Is he out in the pasture?"

"I've looked there. I've looked in every stall in the barn. I checked the horses the students are riding. Did someone leave the gate open? Could he have wandered into the street? Would someone take him!"

Mrs. Kramer couldn't help laughing that her trick had worked on the number one prankster. "Little miss, how does it feel to have someone play a joke on *you*? I hid March Lad. If you go over to the dog kennels, you'll find a rather large surprise."

After that, Margie *tried* to be a little more careful about her pranks, but opportunities just seemed to continue to present themselves.

CHAPTER FIVE

Meanwhile, Back at the Ranch

I TURNED OFF KENDALL DRIVE into the gravel road of Gladewinds Farm. The rocks crunched under the weight of the car as I slowly drove toward the schooling arena in the back. Islands of green pine trees around the periphery of the eighteen to twenty acres swayed in the gentle breeze. The frantic pace of many errands receded from my thoughts as the familiar scenes unfolded.

I smiled as I passed the mare and her yearling in the front pasture. She and her offspring had been the excited center of many carpool conversations. Dinnertime must be approaching for the occupants of the small-animal kennel. The demanding orders of the dogs created a cacophony of barks, yelps, and howls. The distant whinnying in the background added to the barnyard symphony.

The plain wood barn stood clean and tall behind the main building: a home occupied by Dorothy and Bob Kramer and their three daughters, Robin, Janice, and Terry. To the left was a fenced-in area worn bald by the constant trodding of the ponies and their young riders. Slightly to the right of the barn and still behind the Kramer home was an area that included the kennel and the runs used by the cats, dogs, and other small animals.

After parking the car and walking toward the pickup area, I overheard Margie's mentor, Karen, reminding one of the boarders about her forgetfulness. "Hey, Your Highness, you left your saddle in the middle of the barn. There are no servants here. You know where to put it."

"Yes, ma'am," came the snappy reply.

Between house and barn, a group of palm and gumbo-limbo trees with benches underneath served as a welcoming oasis where the students rested after completing their lessons. I greeted the sprawled-out, heat-soaked girls from our carpool and headed for the nearest tree. "Hi, Mrs. Kramer, you've found a nice shady place to escape the summer heat. May I join you?"

"Sure. Your daughter has two more ponies to school after she finishes cooling down Bluey, so you might as well get comfortable."

"Thanks," I said. "And speaking of thanks, Margie's dad and I are sure grateful you're letting her earn extra lessons. Having two sons in college doesn't leave much money for extras."

"Don't thank me," Mrs. Kramer replied. "Both Karen and Penny tell me how Margie's riding has helped make the horses more responsive to their commands. She seems to get inside their heads somehow, or maybe they just know she means business. Whatever it is, she's going to be one of our best riders and trainers soon."

"That's good to hear," I said. "We're glad she's channeling her stubbornness into something so healthy."

Mrs. Kramer looked at me in surprise. "I don't know about 'stubborn.' My husband and I rather like her *determination*. She's finishing up with Holly. Next comes Garnet. You'll see what I mean."

I answered, "Oh, have we heard about Garnet! Margie tell us that not even the professionals can do much with her. Is it true you bet her a can of soda she couldn't stay on Garnet for a whole riding lesson?"

Mrs. Kramer smiled. "You should know if you want Margie to do something, all you have to do is say it's too difficult for her."

It was my turn to smile. "We noticed some extra black-and-blue spots all over her body. When we asked her about them, she told us Garnet likes to stop unexpectedly at one of the jumps."

Mrs. Kramer agreed. "Yes, she sure does. That ornery little creature has perfected the art of stopping short, dropping her shoulder, and promptly dumping the rider. Margie has learned to land on her feet, and Garnet is dumping her fewer times. If they keep improving like this, we'll be entering the two of them in one of the local shows on Saturday."

As I watched the horse and rider finishing their session, I couldn't help but see why Mrs. Kramer was so pleased. My fun-loving, joke-telling daughter who would soon be driving home with me was nowhere to be seen. I was looking at a picture of total attention to the task at hand. Again and again they would repeat the jumps. Every successful hurdle would bring an excited "Good girl!" or an affectionate pat on the neck. When Margie rewarded Garnet with a carrot and began the cooling-down walk, I couldn't help smiling at her soft-spoken words. "That's what I expect, you beautiful little girl. We both know you can do it. You're so-o-o good!"

When she returned all the horses to their stalls, a beaming rider joined the carpool group. Her wet blouse stuck to her skin. Her face was covered with the dust from the schooling ring. One clean streak, where she must have wiped off the perspiration, gleamed from her dirty face. "Okay, gang, what are we waiting for? We're off to see the wizard—the wonderful wizard of Oz," she sang out happily.

"Not so fast, Dorothy," I said, as the fragrance of my daughter assaulted my nostrils. "Wipe your boots over there on the grass. We don't need to bring back souvenirs from Kansas."

CHAPTER SIX

Lessons Learned

MRS. KRAMER WAS TRUE TO HER WORD. When she felt they were ready, Margie and Garnet rode in three consecutive pony hunter and equitation events. As our daughter learned about the world of riding competition, we gained knowledge about the people who inhabited that world.

We both had a lot to learn. Irv had ridden horses when he was a young boy attending camp. I had never even been astride one. Now our daughter's interest was propelling us toward completely new experiences.

The first of the small horse shows arrived on a bright summer day. The air was crisp and bristled with Margie's excitement. We dropped her off at Gladewinds so that she could help prepare the horses and load the trucks with the skittish animals and all the equipment that went with them. With me as navigator, Irv followed the directions Margie had given us. As we drove, we commented on the many horse farms that dotted the landscape in the Kendall area. "I had no idea so many people owned horses. Every home seems to have acres of land as well as barns and stalls," I noted.

When we passed a collection of small stores, Irv added, "Did you see the feed and hay store? That tells you quite a bit about the area."

We located the designated arena, easily sighted by the large number of trailer trucks and horse vans that filled the outer perimeter as well as much of the acreage within the fenced-in farm. We parked on the street and wound our way in and out among the vehicles, owners, horses, and—what seemed to us—an equal number of dogs.

The hubbub of activity encompassed both a joyous we're-at-a-county-fair attitude and a serious, well-performed preparation for the forthcoming event. I found it difficult to identify who was competing. Parent and child were equally busy and identically clad. They wore their jodhpurs and boots with casual elegance and studied indifference.

Someone from this purposeful group must have recognized me—probably from school. "You're Margie's mother?"

I looked at her inquiringly. "Yes."

"If you want to help your daughter," she offered, "you'll see that she dresses herself as well as she grooms her horse."

The shock of her advice must have registered on my face, but I gritted my teeth, faked a smile, and managed a surprised, "Thank you."

"What was that about?" Irv inquired.

"I'm not sure if I was just put down by a snob or if I didn't recognize someone just trying to be helpful. From what I've seen and heard, many of these parents are reliving their days of glory. They traveled the circuit when they were children, and now that their own kids are into show jumping, they take every little detail so-o-o seriously. I like the fact that Margie and her friends are enjoying themselves, learning responsibility, and getting a chance to just be children!"

"What was this about her outfit?"

"I'm not sure. She's wearing the hunt cap and belt that we got her for her tenth birthday. The ratcatcher, jodhpurs, and boots are hand-me-downs from the Kramer daughters."

"What are ratcatchers?"

"Oh, Irv, you know less than I do. That's the special blouse with the attached collar they wear for the horse shows. Evidently, the collarless shirts were worn by British men who killed rats—exterminators."

We finally found our way to the bleachers, where I introduced Irv to a group of fellow carpoolers. We began to relax and converse with the people around us. "Is this Margie's first show?" someone asked.

"Well, she rode Andrea's horse, Sweet Charity, when she was nine, but that was a walk-trot class. This will be her first show where she'll jump over the fences. I'm a little nervous about that."

"Don't worry. The fences in the equitation classes are quite low—only a couple of feet tall. The judges will base their decisions on how smoothly the riders change the horses' stride and how well they maintain their position. They look for style and evenness and form."

I tried to relax. Finally, our daughter cantered onto the field. To our untrained eyes, Margie and Garnet looked great as they successfully jumped the nine hurdles. Later we would learn that Margie was an effective, rather than a pretty, rider. She did not have the height or the long legs, and because she rode such difficult horses, she did what it took to get them over fences. Margie had learned so much on her own and was technically in the right position, but she did not have the finesse some of the well-guided riders exhibited. When our daughter's fans began to cheer, Irv and I exchanged smiles. "Yeah, Margie." "Go, Margie." If she heard, we could not tell from her focused attention: jaws rigid, brown eyes staring toward each hurdle ahead. That stern look always surprised us.

When everyone had completed their course, the judge announced, "And the first-place winner is—Margie Goldstein." I jumped up, grabbed Irv, and the two of us jumped up and down right along with the children.

We approached the second horse show less tentatively. We knew Margie's group of friends and liked each one of them. There was an air of good health, purpose, and enthusiasm about the boys and girls. They pursued their activities with vigor, loved the horses they worked with, and enjoyed an easy familiarity among themselves. They respected one another's accomplishments and applauded long and loud when one of their group performed well. One particularly good performance brought Margie's friends to their feet as they shouted out their appreciation. "Who is *that*?" we overheard.

"One of the *Gladewinds* group," came a condescending explanation.

We ignored such pettiness and concentrated on the activities, the children's pride, and the outfits representing their unique sport. Regulation dress was worn as much for safety as for style. The hunt cap was not just jaunty, but also made of hard plastic to ensure as much protection as possible. Jodhpurs narrowed at the lower leg to prevent wrinkles, and the suede on the inside of the thighs and down the inside knee and calf helped the rider grip the horse. The leather boots allowed the rider a firmer grip around the horse, and the attached spurs provided the incentive to move forward. If a rider fell, the strength of the boots offered further protection should the horse step on him or her.

One of the children's relatives in our Gladewinds group commented, "I can't help noticing that somehow the horses look better than their riders."

This time I was prepared. "Isn't it great? I think they just love those horses so much, they spend extra time grooming them. Margie may not be immaculate, but her horse sure is."

The afternoon competition ended, and once again Margie won a blue ribbon.

By the time we attended the third show, we felt very knowledgeable about what to expect. Even Margie's winning the blue ribbon for the third time seemed to be part of the routine, so we were taken off guard by the remark of one of our group.

"If that were my child, I'd find the most expensive horse available and buy it for her." I don't even remember what I replied, but I had to remind myself that she was saying this in recognition of Margie's skill. Our financial priorities were completely unknown to most of the people in this world of relative wealth.

At the end of the third show, her dad and I expected to see a joyous victor.

"What's the matter, honey. You *won*, remember?"

"Oh, I'm happy about *that*, but now Garnet will be sold for a better price so that the Kramers can buy more ponies for the students. I'll miss her so much." Her lips quivered as she struggled for control. We gave her a hug of understanding as she tried to deal with this bittersweet moment.

"Margie, if we could buy you a horse, we would." Our voices trailed off as she quickly interrupted us.

"I know. I know. I'll see you soon after I finish loading the horses on the trailer."

* * *

We attended additional horse shows and observed the close communication between horse and rider. "Honey, I know you use your legs to guide the horses. We can't help seeing how muscular your thighs are becoming. How else do you guide them?"

"Mom, to make it real simple—think of the hands to guide the front end and the legs to control the back end."

"Okay, I've got that. Now, what do you do specifically with each end?"

"The hands are mostly on the reins, which are connected to the bit in the horse's mouth. You pull the reins to tell the horse which direction to go. If you want him to go right, you pull right. If you want him to go left, you pull the reins to the left."

"I can understand that. How do you get him started? You can't turn on the ignition."

Eleven-year-old Margie rolled her eyes. "You sure you want to know?"

"I really do. How do you get him moving?"

"When you squeeze your calves and heels together, you channel him forward. For the less sensitive ones and only if needed, you use spurs. Your legs can help him with directions also. At the same time as you're pulling the reins to make him go left, you press your right leg to his side. When you want to turn right, you direct him right with your reins and press him with the left leg."

"Margie, that's a lot more complicated than I realized. Anything else we should watch for?"

"You know when you see me petting the horse after we go over the hurdles?" Margie continued. "They're like babies. They need reassurance and praise. Also, since they can't tell us how they feel, we have to know whether they're afraid or stubborn."

"Isn't that hard to know?" I wondered.

"That's why I like to ride so many different kinds of horses. Each one is different. Garnet was so ornery that I had to be real firm with her when she was bad and give her lots of treats when she did well. March Lad is so eager to please that I have to be more gentle so he doesn't get discouraged. Really, after a while, you get a horse sense for what they're thinking and can feel what they feel."

The more shows we watched, the more we understood Margie's love and pride in her four-legged friends—and the more we learned as well. We now knew that the size of the horse determined the division. The steed was measured from the top of the front hoof to the withers, at the end of the neck, right above the shoulder. The measuring stick was calibrated in "hands," and each hand equaled four inches. Because of Margie's small size, the Kramers and others wanted her to ride in pony divisions. If the horse measured 12.2 hands or under, she rode in a small-pony class; 12.2 to 13.2 hands were medium ponies; 13.2 to 14.2 were considered large ponies.

The Gladewinds group especially loved the little local shows that took place at some of the farms in the southwestern part of Miami, at the South Miami Riding Club right next to Baptist Hospital, or at Tropical Park on Bird Road. These informal events, unrated by the American Horse Show Association (AHSA—at the time, the overall governing body for all horse shows), provided competition but mostly fun. Often the children would ride the ponies along little-traveled (at *that* time!) Kendall Drive, followed by adults in cars, all headed for an exciting weekend show. Once there, they worked out of vehicles that held vast amounts of equipment.

The gymkhana shows gave the riders an opportunity to work as a team, and the members of the Gladewinds group were loud and hearty as they cheered one another through the different relay races. At the end of a show, Margie would bounce into the house: "I won a bar of saddle soap. That means I have more money from my allowance to buy some treats for the ponies." Sometimes she won oil for the reins or a special grooming brush. These practical items were regarded as treasures on a par with the gold bars of Fort Knox.

Gradually, as their skills increased, the Gladewinds riders entered shows with AHSA judges and stewards. These official representatives were there to solve problems, answer questions, and ensure that the rules were followed.

"Mom, Dad, these judges didn't like March Lad. I thought he went really well in the pony hunter class and they didn't even notice."

"Which one was the hunter class?" I asked.

"That's the one where they judge strictly on the horse. Remember I told you? In the equitation, they judge the rider's position and effectiveness, but with hunter it's strictly the pony or horse—how well he moves, his jumping style, how smooth he looks."

"Did March Lad follow all your signals?"

"He was great! I'd signal him for a walk, a trot, or a canter, and he'd respond immediately. And did you see him go over the cross-rail fence? He lifted his legs nice and high, and Bobbi said his back was arched perfectly when we made the jump. I'm not sure the judge noticed, though. He always seemed to be looking at someone else when he gave the voice commands."

"So it's strictly the judge's opinion who wins?"

"Yeah. I can't wait until I'm big enough for jumpers. You either go over the fence or you don't. That seems more fair to me."

"Well, Margie, *I* can wait! Besides, no one wins all the time."

Margie shook her head from side to side. "I know. I know. But I sure do wish the judge liked March Lad as much as *I* do."

Sometimes the shows began so early, the children slept at the barn so they could begin the many hours of preparation. We stopped by Gladewinds on our way to a horse show. "Margie, didn't you just bathe and groom March Lad yesterday?"

"Sure did. But they have to just *shine* on the day of a show."

Laddie (his nickname or barn name) decided this was a perfect time for a little horseplay and turned around to take Margie's sunglasses right off her face. "Not now, Laddie. We've got too much to do."

She continued brushing Laddie's chestnut coat. He took the opportunity to untie her shoes. "Oh, Laddie, you're such a brat." Her tone clearly indicated she thought he was the cleverest little animal she had ever encountered.

One day in the summer of 1970, Margie announced, "Mom, I'll have to be at the farm an hour earlier this Saturday."

"Why is that?"

"You know who George Morris is? I've shown you the articles he writes in my horse magazines. He's so fa-a-mous! Mrs. Kramer is sponsoring a clinic for the Gladewinds students—she's paying for me—and I can't

A twelve-year-old Margie began training and showing Gladewinds's March Lad, who became Champion Large Pony of Florida. Laddie, a large pony (half Arabian, half Welsh), was very smart and rather playful. He learned to untie shoes and take off Margie's sunglasses and watch. Margie taught him to lunge with no lunge line, walk, trot, and canter by voice command. He was easy to ride and highly successful. Photographer: *Doug Leaky*

believe he's going to teach us! It's so exciting to have someone who's known and respected all over the world, and he's coming *here*. Would you believe he won the team gold medal in the 1955 Pan Am Games and the team silver medal in the 1960 Olympics? And he's coached other Olympic gold medalists like Leslie Burr, Conrad Homfeld, and Joe Fargis." The wonder in her voice was palpable.

"Okay, honey. If you're that excited, we can get up an hour earlier. Does Mrs. Kramer plan many of these clinics?"

"During the next year, she's scheduled Carl Bessett for a couple more sessions. He's one of the country's top show-jumping instructors, and we have some other top trainers—it's a real privilege to ride in front of them!"

These lessons from the experts spurred twelve-year-old Margie's horse knowledge and pursuit of excellence even further. "You sure are learning a lot. What else is going on?"

"Well, Mrs. Kramer likes me to watch the farrier—that's the blacksmith—when he shoes the horses. The horses often need new shoes every three and a half to six weeks."

"That's not very long."

"Sometimes the ponies grow fast and sometimes they just wear them out or lose them. The angles have to be correct or it throws them off balance and it affects the tendons or the shoulder muscles. She says you really must have a good blacksmith or you can ruin a good horse."

"Margie, I'm astounded at what you're learning! Is there more that Mrs. Kramer is teaching you?"

"Yes, she's taking me with her when she buys new horses. She's teaching me what to look for when you buy them."

"Goodness, she *does* have faith in you. What exactly do you look for?"

"You look at their soundness, elasticity of stride, conformation, how they move—some are more athletic than others—and if we want to use them right away for the school students, I ride them to see how well they follow commands and how good their temperament is."

I felt very knowledgeable the next time we went to a horse show and enjoyed sharing the information with Irv. He immediately asked another question that fortunately was answered by one of the more experienced Gladewinds parents. "If the course is posted just prior to the event, how can the riders remember all that so they can signal their horses?"

"A good memory is one of the skills a competitor needs. They have to know the order of the hurdles as well as how to jump over them. Besides, they have an opportunity right before the event to walk the course and pace off the distances between obstacles."

We were learning.

Horse shows gradually became routine for Irv and me—and unfortunately so did accidents. We had rushed the boys to the emergency room or to the pediatrician often enough that we could remain relatively calm as they were stitched up or as they had bones reset. We could do no less for our daughter, so we fought the desire to take away her beloved activity.

This worry of ours must have been very much on young Margie's mind. Sherri Cicero told us—many years *after* the event—about her first words when she was thrown from a horse and knocked unconscious. As her eyes began to flutter and she was just reviving, she grabbed her best friend's arm and said, "You didn't let them call my mother, did you?" Concussions, casts on her arm or leg—she would allow nothing to stop her from going to the barn.

"Irv, do you ever get the idea our daughter is manipulating us?"

"Only if we let her. We'll just have to watch carefully to see if she's hurting."

When Margie had competed in horse shows for about two years, we heard more and more about a pony named Angelwings. "Angel has the most beautiful eyes. When I talk to her, I know she understands. Will you come to watch me this Sunday? You'll see how cute she is and how well she responds."

Showtime arrived. Irv and I observed from the stands. We were aware of Margie's preparation: the time spent on oiling the reins and bridle, polishing the stirrups, brushing the horse, braiding the mane and tail.

As she took her turn in the ring, we stared in horror. Time froze. The pony sharply veered in one direction, and Margie—still clutching the slippery reins—slid in the opposite direction. She seemed to float in the air before she fell to the hard earth below. The fear caught in my throat, and I could barely swallow. We rushed in panic to where Margie lay.

Before we could utter a sound, we heard our daughter barely push out the words, "Mom, Dad. That was an emergency dismount."

Later when we were alone, I lamented to my husband, "I don't know whether to laugh or cry."

"I know what you mean. She knows our ambivalence toward her hobby, and her first thought was to reassure *us*. What a girl!"

That night in the quiet of our bedroom, the two of us once again debated whether to allow our daughter to continue riding. Although Margie had always insisted the only time there were accidents were when she herself was acting the daredevil or taking too great a chance, the worry for her physical well-being was constant.

"She already has had a concussion, broken shoulder, broken arm, and twisted ankle. Next time it could be worse."

"But how many other not-yet-thirteen-year-old-children have her sense of responsibility and willingness to work toward a goal?"

"It's too much. She could have been paralyzed today!"

"You take a chance in everything you do in life. Look how compassionate she is with others and how confident she is already!"

Back and forth. Pro and con. It was a discussion that would be repeated many times over the years.

CHAPTER SEVEN

Juggling 101

MARGIE BENEFITED FROM HAVING MARK AND EDDIE AS OLDER SIBLINGS. We saw the humor—as well as the horror—of the teenage years. We felt that raising children at this time in their lives was a little like navigating through a minefield on horseback. We tried our best to guide our horses through the dangers, but with every misstep we expected an explosion.

Because of his temperment, Mark presented few problems. He had many interests and was an extremely mature child. Even as a young boy, he would question what he didn't understand; after receiving the information, he would reply, "Okay, that's reasonable." When he reached the teen years, he simply buried himself further into his books, his award-winning projects, and his many hobbies. We worried only slightly about his shyness around girls, noting that this seemed to be typical of his friends as well.

Eddie's playful and impetuous nature often brought on unexpected consequences. Mark, at sixteen, had left home for college, leaving fourteen-year-old Eddie and seven-year-old Margie. We no sooner walked out of the house for an evening than our younger two went to work. "Think you're good enough to play one-on-one football with me, Margie?"

"Eddie, you're seven years older than I am."

"Okay, let's make it even. I'll play on my knees."

The fierce competitors would be so involved in the game that soon Ed's knees began to bleed or something would be broken. One of our favorite wedding gifts, a small ceramic mother and child, became the usual casualty. I repaired it repeatedly until there was nothing left to mend.

This horseplay of our children often erupted spontaneously. "Eddie, Margie, we're going in the back to get dressed. Don't forget your after-dinner chores."

"Sure."

"No problem."

Within seconds, the wet sponges or the soapy water flew at the intended target. Then one or the other would look for a tactical advantage. Taking the high ground—literally—Margie would climb atop the cupboards and "bomb" Eddie below. They had it timed perfectly. Before we exited our bedroom, the mopping and cleaning up had been completed. As we left the house for the evening, we'd call out, "Great job!" Only when they reached adulthood did we find out how this had been accomplished. Their code of silence and loyalty to each other remained a constant throughtout all the years of their childhood.

When Margie reached her teens, we braced ourselves for an explosion that never detonated.

"Sometimes I'm amazed, Irv," I told my husband. "We'll be talking and she'll suddenly tell me she has to go to her room. She says that if we keep on discussing whatever it is we're talking about, we'll be arguing soon. She'll stay by herself until the mood passes, and then she'll come out as if nothing has happened."

"Well, you can't complain about that, Mona."

"I'm not. I just find it absolutely amazing that she can *feel* the change in her mood and leave before we end up with angry words. I talk to the other mothers of teenagers—especially female teenagers—and they do nothing but fight."

"Do you think it's because the horses are such a big incentive? She's so focused and much too happy to want to get into arguments. Or maybe she's just concerned about being grounded."

"Could be. She told me her science class was discussing drug abuse, and her teacher said, 'Margie, you're too high on life with the animals to get involved with stimulants.' Which reminds me, our neighbor down the block has dropped out of the Gladewinds carpool. Her interest in horses wasn't strong enough to keep her from being both boy crazy and drug crazy as well."

Irv said, "I hope our keeping the lines of communication open and her seeing that we practice what we preach has helped her."

"I do, too. I've been thinking. She's so close to the older girls. When they tell her the exact same thing we do, it's as if The Word has come down from the mountain. Remember how upset she was when she picked up a wrong lead on one of the green horses she was riding for one of Bibby's pupils? Bibby just looked at her and said, 'No, you did *not* let the owners down. It happens. Stop being so hard on yourself.' If I told her that, she'd tell me I don't understand. When they tell her, she takes it to heart."

"Well, whatever the reason, we should be grateful and try not to worry so much about her staying in one piece." Little did we know how futile those words would be.

"Margie, your dad and I received a wedding invitation from Karen also. That was mighty nice of her."

"That's Karen. I wish she could have met Mark. She would make a *great* sister-in-law."

"Margie, you sure like to hold on to your friends! Is she going to continue out at the barn?"

"She's already planning on a family. She won't be traveling as much, but she'll continue giving lessons."

The wedding was lovely. The bronzed and beautiful bride and groom could have stepped from an advertisement. After the church ceremony, everyone convened in Karen's mother's house and the festivities began. Cameras flashed. Old friends shouted greetings. Laughter floated through the crowd.

The photographer tried to call out his instructions over the excited celebrants. "Karen, it's time to throw your garter. Lift your dress and let your new husband . . ."

He didn't get to finish his sentence. Everyone standing near the happy couple was laughing heartily. Karen, who had disappeared for only a few moments earlier, lifted her long dress, raised her leg, and exposed not a shapely calf and thigh—but well-worn paddock boots!

On the way home, our daughter mused about the proceedings. "Wasn't that great! When I get married, I'll have to remember my boots also!"

Now that Margie attended the upper grades in public school, making time for all her activities required much planning. She knew we placed a great value on her school achievement, and she pursued her education and the extracurricular activies without any reminders from us. She never missed her chores and joys at the barn no matter the weather, the day, or the difficulty with transportation. Somehow, Margie always found the time.

She also found out how to deal with devastating loss.

"Mom, Dad, why did this happen to Mrs. Kramer? It's just not fair!"

"What do you mean, Margie?"

"Janice told me her mother has bone cancer. I tried to talk to Mr. Kramer, but he won't answer me. He looks so sad. I just don't know what to do."

When Mrs. Kramer, truly a second mother to Margie, spent her final months bedridden, Margie found it increasingly difficult to face the daily routine. Yet she started every afternoon at the farm with a visit to Mrs. Kramer's bedroom.

"You're going to get better. I want you—I *need* you—to be better."

"Margie, when have we been anything but honest with one another? When I'm gone, promise me you'll help with Terry. My two older girls will be all right, but Terry's so young, only twelve. She looks up to you."

"Of course I will. I—I—" She couldn't get the words out. She retreated into happier memories. "Remember when you hid March Lad from me? I was so afraid he had gotten loose and we'd lost him."

"Well, you certainly brought that on yourself, young lady. With all the jokes you've played on everyone, you can hardly complain about one prank. No more playing with firecrackers, though—that's just too dangerous, even if you think you can handle everything."

"Mrs. Kramer, I was *much* younger then."

"Last week?"

All Margie could manage was a shaky smile. "That was last year on the Fourth of July."

"I'm getting very tired now. Before you leave, would you hand me my medicine and a glass of water? And I have something for you. Gladewinds will live forever, Margie, because I'm *giving* the name to you. I know you'll never bring anything but honor to it."

Moving mechanically as if in a trance, the distraught young girl brought the requested items, handed over the pills, then held the glass for additional support. When this small task was completed, she stood by the door, hesitated, and struggled with the words she'd been unable to say a few minutes before: "Mrs. Kramer, I—I—I love you!"

Margie raced across the field and into the barn. Fortunately, everyone was busy elsewhere, and she could allow the tears to flow down her cheeks without fear of being seen. Her vision blurred, she nearly tripped over a bucket of feed. Angrily she kicked at the offending object and received a sore toe for her effort. She saddled the horse, stroked his mane, and repeated to him over and over, "It's just not fair. It's just not fair." That afternoon, she rode the steed until both were exhausted.

Mrs. Kramer had given the heartbroken young girl so much more than a name. She also gave her love, trust, and the strength to say good-bye when the time came.

After Mrs. Kramer died, Margie took her daughter Terry under her wing, and they traveled the Florida horse show circuit with the rest of the Gladewinds "family." "My wife wanted you to have this," stammered Mr. Kramer as he handed the sixteen-year-old girl a brand-new saddle. "And I'm giving you my credit card and the keys to the truck and trailer. Don't you take no guff from those kids." He tried to hide his generosity behind his harsh words.

Off they went. Margie matched appropriate-level shows with herself and Terry and many of the other younger riders. She sent off for descriptions, prize lists, and entry forms, and gained much experience in the smaller shows. In addition to participating in their own divisions, the Gladewinds group always found time to watch their heroes at the Grand Prix events. Margie absorbed every bit of knowledge she could by observing the competitions and by grooming for different professionals to learn the techniques and individual styles and skills of the top riders.

"Wasn't Katie Monahan wonderful at the Tampa show?" "Did you see the way Joe Fargis turned his horse in such a tight area? Do you think any of us will ever be in an AGA show?" After watching a Grand Prix in Palm Beach or Tampa, they even wrote and sang songs that described their heroes' accomplishments. Meanwhile, they were not only setting goals for themselves, but also forging friendships that would last throughout the years.

By 1974, Margie rode in the junior hunter division, which—at the bigger shows—was divided by the size of the mounts. Small junior hunters were defined as those measuring 14.2 to 16 hands, while those over 16 hands were considered to be large junior hunters. The "really big guys" were yet to come.

The biggest challenge to Margie's carefully worked-out routine occurred in her senior year of high school. Because her school was so crowded, there were three shifts for every grade. "I'll never have enough time to ride all the horses," she grumbled. "If I had either morning or afternoon, I'd have half a day to ride! With the shift in the middle, there's not enough time in the morning or the afternoon."

"You're right. I've written a letter to the committee that oversees requests for schedule changes. Hopefully, they'll understand."

When that didn't work, I tried again. "Margie, your counselor agrees with us, but says there's nothing we can do. All this has taken time and we're now past the deadline. Any suggestions?"

"Mom, I met one of my friend's aunts. She's a nurse and has to go by Gladewinds if we can get to her house by five thirty in the morning."

"Margie, do you realize that we'll have to wake up at five o'clock—five days a week until the end of the school year!—so we can eat breakfast and do all the things we need to do to get you there on time?"

At five twenty in the morning with our moods as somber and dark as the early hour, we drove to her benefactor's house. Then I went home to finish dressing while Margie was relayed to the barn. Since it was still so dark, she had to wait until the sun rose before she could ride. Sometimes, when she had many horses to school, she even started as the sun's first dim promise of light peeked across the horizon. She left in time to take a bus home, shower, dress, and then arrive promptly for eleven o'clock classes at South Miami Senior High School. What a celebration we had when that year ended!

"Margie, how is your schedule working out at Miami Dade Community College?" I asked.

"I can't believe how understanding my instructors are! One of my professors saw the Tampa horse show on ESPN and he asked so many questions. He has a daughter who loves horses and he wanted to know mainly about the safety of riding such large animals. In fact, he wanted me to teach her."

"That's great, honey, but you still are trying to do too much. How are you feeling physically?"

"Fine" came her too-quick reply. "My math prof wants to know how we estimate the number of strides between the jumps. When I explained about our pacing the course on foot, then converting it to number of horse strides, he used the information in some of his mathematical equations."

"Good for him! I like to hear about teachers who relate their instruction to practical concerns. What do you do about tests? How do you get your homework turned in on time?"

"Mom, don't worry. I've worked a schedule out with each of my teachers. Sometimes I take a test before I leave town. Same thing with my homework—that can be done in advance. If they spring any surprises on the class while I'm on the road, I'm handed the same surprise the minute I walk through the door. As I said, they've really been great!"

As Margie completed her courses with her usual diligence, we tried not to be so concerned about her full days and nights. She was going to college from 7 A.M. till noon, then straight to the stable to ride until dark. In order to maintain her 4.0 average, she spent the entire evening on her homework. The tired look in her eyes and the missing bounce from her step kept nagging at our attempted calm. "We just don't like the way you're dragging. I've called the doctor and we have an appointment on Friday. Sorry, honey, but this is a done deal." When Margie did *not* argue, we really worried!

The conference with her physician proceeded as we expected. "Young lady, your blood work confirms my diagnosis. You have a severe case of mononucleosis. Since we have no medicine to combat the disease, our only treatment is complete bed rest. In your case, I'd estimate at least six months before you can even try to return to any part of your routine."

For three months, the only time our daughter even tried to lift her head was to acknowledge a friend's visit or to eat—what seemed to us—a pitifully small portion of food.

One morning, Bobbi Badgley came for a visit. I heard them talking and felt good that Margie's voice sounded a little stronger. When I came in to see if the girls needed anything, I could not believe my eyes. There was my patient, fully dressed in her barn clothes, ready to go. "Margie, what do you think you're doing?"

"Mom, Bobbi is driving me out to the barn. Carole is depending on me to get her ready for an important horse show. I can't disappoint her."

"And what about us? We're worried about you enough without having you disregard doctor's orders! Please, Margie, don't do this to yourself. You could end up staying out even *longer* than six months!"

Neither of us convinced the other. As the two girls started to walk out the door, I turned to Bobbi and managed a feeble, "Would you bring her home when you see she's weakening?"

"I'm not happy about this either, but you know your daughter. She's the most stubborn person I know."

Perhaps her stubbornness gave her strength, but Margie did manage to return gradually to both her studies and her horse routine without the expected relapse. When she received her associate's degree from Miami Dade Community College, she promptly enrolled in the fall classes at Florida International University.

"Whoa, honey, are you sure you can handle all this? You're riding and showing full time. Maybe you can delay one or the other, but college and horse training together are just too much. Are you willing to stay this busy?"

"If I don't take a full load, I can do both, but I won't finish in two years."

"Margie, just remember what the doctor said about your health. You've had mononucleosis once, and he said it was caused probably by overwork. You need to cut back."

"I'm trying. Karen, Bibby, and Penny are sharing the workload with me, and that helps. Besides, my psychology classes are fascinating, and the business courses will be invaluable when I eventually set up my own business."

"And what business is that? What if you became a dental hygentist? You'll be able to set your own hours and still have time for this hobby you love so much."

"Yuck, I can't imagine having to work in people's mouths all day."

"Considering what you've raked from the barns, I think that might be an improvement." I ignored the rueful look headed my way and continued. "Margie, you have such a wonderful way with children. How about teaching as a career? You'll have weekends and the summer to ride the horses."

During these years, her father and I worried about a career that would meet Margie's unusual needs and tried to guide her selection. We had no idea that training and showing horses was anything more than a wonderful hobby.

"Can you build a future with where you're headed? We know you enjoy what you're doing, that you're able to make money from both your lessons and showing horses, but you have to be practical. You need a career that will let you be self-supporting."

In an effort to prove exactly what she could do and that she already was directed toward an occupation, Margie announced one day that she already had paid her college tuition.

"Margie, there's no way we'll allow you to pay for your education. If we can do this for your brothers, we certainly can do it for you. Here's a check. Thanks for the offer, but we'll hear no more on the subject!"

If Margie couldn't spend her money one way, she spent it another. She lived at home and was able to put money in the bank every week. She drove our hand-me-down automobiles from the time she first started college and found them to be reliable and serviceable. One afternoon she rolled into our circular drive, a beaming smile on her face as she summoned us to see her first major purchase. "How do you like my new car?" she asked proudly.

"Margie, it's beautiful! You sure bought yourself a sporty number."
We looked at the Pontiac Fiero, a low-slung two-seater with its sleek exterior molded entirely in plastic, and added, "Where are you going to put all the equipment you normally carry?"

She opened the door, pushed the driver's seat forward, and—sure enough—she had squeezed in her saddle, reins, bridle, boots, hunt cap, and all the usual paraphernalia she needed. When she opened the trunk, she showed us her portable "office." There were all the files and records that she used in her daily travels. Margie covered many miles and several counties during each day. She had clients from Homestead all the way up to West Palm Beach, and she either taught them or rode their horses at the owners' barns. "Use it well, honey," we added as we continued to express our admiration.

Margie delighted in that little car for many years, until it came to an unusual end.

"The horse ate *what*?" the insurance adjuster asked increduously.

"The horse ate about one-third of the top of my car. I had parked it outside the fenced-in pasture under a tree. When I finished all my lessons—which were on the other side of the barn so none of us saw him—I came out and there was my car in shreds."

"Wait till I tell the guys in the main office about this!" Margie laughed when she told us how completely amazed he sounded.

After a short time of driving her patched-up automobile, the next car she purchased was built of metal.

The children whom Margie taught to ride and jump were often from a privileged background. They had few responsibilities for themselves, much less for a large four-legged animal. They found Margie to be a hard taskmaster, but a fair one. She allowed no temper tantrums or neglect of the horses in any way. Usually she could find something to laugh about with her pupils and turned their times together into joyous occasions. Sometimes the lessons simply stressed both teacher and pupil.

"Mom, Dad, you wouldn't believe the tantrum Tom threw today when I was teaching him. His horse didn't respond to his commands, so he stormed off, left the horse in the ring, threw his hat across the field, and just sulked. His mother asked him what the matter was and he started screaming at her."

"What did you say to him, Margie?"

"I let him know that there was no way I would continue teaching him if he couldn't learn to control *himself* and not take out his anger on the horse. I told him that I wouldn't give him lessons if he didn't talk to me and his mother with respect."

"How did his mother react to that?"

"Well, at first she started to make excuses for him, but when she saw how serious I was, she backed me up."

The day following this event, Tom called to apologize. A few months later, Margie received a gift and a letter from Tom's mother: "I'm so proud of my son's progress. It's not just that he's riding better—he's so much nicer to be around! Even his teachers at school have commented on his respect and responsibility. Margie, his father and I can't thank you enough!"

Irv and I treasured the letters from her pupils' parents that told of the impact she had on their children's lives. We were so proud when we went to horse shows and were told about the skills and values Margie taught their sons and daughters. As far as we were concerned, she was reinforcing good character traits in herself as well.

Listening to my daughter sharing success stories about her pupils really gave me great pleasure. Each child is so different, and finding the one best approach or combination of approaches is quite a challenge. Whether you're teaching them how to compute or read, as I was doing, or teaching them how to ride a horse as Margie was, the goals required the same techniques.

We met Carole when she came to Miami, so we understood the difficulties facing Margie, who was only a few years older than her student. Carole was bright, pretty, and personable. She also was not used to listening well to others. Perhaps because her right arm ended at the elbow, her parents tried to compensate for this birth defect by granting their daughter everything she wanted.

Carole wanted Margie as her teacher, and she got Margie as her teacher—even though they had to fly her into Fort Myers in their private plane. The lessons were often intense.

"Carole, you're not giving the horse a clear signal with the reins. Try pulling a little harder in the direction you want him to go."

"I can't. I can't give enough with the left rein."

"Yes, you can. Turn your body slightly inward on the left side to give more with that rein."

"I can't, I can't," wailed Carole as the tears began to flow.

"Get down from the horse and watch what I'm going to do." Margie showed her rider what she expected. "Okay, now it's your turn. I'll work with your problem, but I don't want you to use it as an excuse not to try."

Each time Margie returned from Fort Myers, we heard the story of how much progress her pupil had made and how much self-confidence she was developing. When Carole won the title of Florida's Champion Jumper Rider in the junior division, two families in Florida—one in Miami, one in Fort Meyers—rejoiced in her accomplishment. Margie had won this title a few years earlier, but the pride in her pupil overshadowed even her own victory.

CHAPTER EIGHT

The Road to Success
Is Not Always Paved

IN ADDITION TO TEACHING THE YOUNGER CHILDREN AT GLADEWINDS, Margie was also running a "traveling summer camp" for them. When Karen, Penny, or Bibby was responsible for the younger ones who accompanied them on the summer circuit, Margie often had tried their patience.

"The rug is soaked. Enough of the dueling water pistols."

"The hotel management is complaining that there's shaving cream in the hallways."

"No more pillow fights. There are feathers all over the room."

Once, it had been Margie who was forever the culprit, but now was a different matter. Margie was in her late teens, assuming more responsibility, and she knew every trick that had ever been tried. Irv and I couldn't help smiling as our daughter explained to us how she had to be a proper role model for "her kids." Under her semi-strict guidance, Margie's students still managed to have fun. Yet, as Karen reminisced, "What a relief to be welcomed by the hotels, and not told to find other accommodations!"

We came home one night to see Margie preparing for one of these trips. She was surrounded with paper: an atlas, the show schedules, and the entry forms. We asked, "Where are you going for this trip?"

"Oh, we'll be in Virginia. By the end of the summer, we'll be headed farther north. As soon as I can, I'll give you the schedule."

Margie was truly learning geography firsthand. Additionally, she was learning how to drive a truck, change tires, order feed in advance, reserve the proper accommodations for the traveling troupe in barn or hotel as needed, and handle finances.

"Margie, if you want help from me, you're going to keep complete records!" Irv said.

"Dad, really, you just don't understand. Everybody deals in cash at the horse shows. My clients pay me and I pay for the stalls, the hay, and the entry fees. It's so much easier."

"Easier, but only for the short run! How will you be able to list your expenses when you itemize them for income tax purposes?"

"Income tax? Why do I have to pay income tax?" Margie wondered.

"Margie, whether you like it or not, you have a partner—Uncle Sam. Look, honey, show jumping may be your business, but accounting is mine. What I tell my clients is this: Do it the right way! If you do it the way you're supposed to, then you never have to look over your shoulder. Furthermore, where are your receipts? I see charges from your credit company, but no bills that you've saved."

"That's their business. Of course they're right."

Irv could not believe what he heard, and struggled to contain his frustration. "Margie, people make mistakes. Don't you understand I'm trying to save you money? Hold on to your receipts and give them to me before the monthly statements arrive. I'll check them, and at the end of the year, we'll use them as legitimate business expenses."

"Dad, if that's the way it has to be, I'll try. But I'm going to have to take much more time—which I just don't have—to do what you want."

As time passed, Margie always found the paperwork to be the least appealing part of her career. To her credit, she did try, but the record keeping remained a constant source of contention between her and her father for many years. As for me, I continued to worry about her physical well-being, noting the constant redness on her inner thighs from riding forty, fifty, or sixty horses a day.

In an effort to save money both for herself and for her students, Margie bought a secondhand truck to transport the horses. Proudly she painted

GLADEWINDS FARM across the truck's panels. She owned no barn, no stalls, no land, as well as no horses of her own, but Margie's career was up and running. Well, almost running.

Even though she constantly upgraded her rig and its various automotive parts, one thing or another was always breaking down. Each new piece of transportation seemed to have its own problems, and of course, the truck perversely seemed to fall apart just when it was farthest from the place of purchase. Also, there was the difficulty of having Margie drive the truck down winding mountain roads. We worried constantly at the thought of nineteen-year-old, ninety-five-pound Margie trying to control a multi-ton rig as gravity hurtled her forward.

The horrifying stories were always told many months *after* the fact to avoid parental concern. "The fuel pump broke when we were driving in Tennessee. I was underneath the truck when a policeman stopped. You should have seen his face when I climbed out!" He had taken one look at the five-foot-one-inch Margie, shaken his head in amazement, and provided the name of the nearest service station. Reassured that she had the situation under control, he departed.

A year later, we were glad to hear that twenty-year-old Margie had acquired a partner for the transportation duties. Fortunately, friends or parents of her students had always been willing to share driving time or form part of a cooperative truck convoy.

"Who will be helping you drive when you go to the horse shows this week?" we inquired.

"Oh, you've met Steve Engle. Remember—the veterinarian intern?"

"Mm-hm, you've been dating quite a few nice young men. Which one is he?"

"The one I played tennis with—the tall one."

Irv and I exchanged glances. We compared reactions when we were alone. "Considering that Steve is over six feet tall and Margie's so short, he does stand out, Mona."

"Well, I remember him from the tennis date. Lean. Muscular. Do you realize that was the first time she didn't go to the barn on a Sunday or *anytime*? He must be pretty special!"

Another out-of-town horse show arrived, and we received the same answer to our query about her driving partner.

"Steve is going to help you drive this week also? Isn't he extremely busy with his own career as a vet? You did tell us he puts in ten to twelve hours a day at work. How does he find the time?"

"He flies to where we are and then helps me with driving the truck and horse rig. Oh, and did I tell you? He's my financial partner in the transportation business."

Once again, we heard about their adventures many years after the fact. With Margie as navigator and Steve as driver of their six-horse gooseneck trailer, they headed east toward Roanoke, West Virginia. They had a full load, and everything was proceeding according to plan.

"Steve, the map shows a new four-lane highway going through the mountains. Perhaps we could save a little time with this route," Margie suggested.

"I sure wouldn't mind that. Use the CB radio and see what the truckers in the eighteen-wheelers have to say about road conditions."

"They said they don't know of any problems." For the next fifty miles, as they drove the smooth new highway, Margie conversed and exchanged jokes with the truckers.

Steve looked at the road ahead and said, "Uh-oh, what happened to the highway? All we've got is two narrow lanes, and look! The mountain road is getting steeper. I'm used to Florida and Texas, where it's *flat*." At first, he kept the conversation light, but his knuckles tightened on the steering wheel as driving became increasingly difficult.

Every time they descended, the eighteen-wheelers drew dangerously closer. Margie asked anxiously, "What's happening? Why are those trucks right on our tail?"

"They're trying to save their brakes, which I wish we could do. Our truck has automatic transmission. Every time I try to gear down, the clutch slips and jumps into the next gear."

For the next three hours, Steve fought the forces of gravity. As the mountains became steeper, his brake use became greater. Navigator and driver spoke little. Margie watched as Steve gripped the wheel. She noted his shaky legs as he pressed ever harder on the brakes. She listened to the scrambling noises the horses made as they reacted to the sharp turns and the unsteady pace of the ride. She heard Steve swear softly whenever an eighteen-wheeler once again came around a switchback at the same time they did. Although the temperature was cool, the two of them were drenched in perspiration.

"Margie, I think we can relax soon. I see a four-lane highway up ahead."

Their temporary relief was shattered as a voice on the radio shouted, "Shut her down, man. You're on fire!"

With complete disbelief, Steve looked into the rearview mirror. Margie twisted in her seat to confirm the warning. Flames were leaping from under the trailer. The terrified horses whinnied their confusion. Steve pulled off the road. Everything seemed to be happening at once. Margie jumped out of the truck, ran to the trailer, and tried to calm the horses. Steve turned off the gas and headed toward the fire. The trucker behind them had pulled up behind Steve and was spraying the blaze with his fire extinguisher.

When the flames died down, they assessed the damage. The trailer and horses were unharmed. What used to be their rear axle, however, was now a glowing red-hot piece of metal. All the constant braking had taken its toll on the bearings and caused the fire. Margie and Steve stood on top of a mountain in the middle of the night with no place to go for help.

The helpful trucker offered a suggestion. "There's a kind-of truck stop about fifteen miles down the road. Would you like me to drop you there?"

The tense travelers considered their options. "We can't leave the horses in the middle of nowhere, Steve." But Margie knew that he was not about to let her go off with some stranger—nor would he want her to stay alone.

"Thanks for all your help. We'll both go with you," Steve replied to the trucker.

As promised, a small undistinguished building, giving few hints to its function, presented a welcome sight for the broken-down travelers. They entered a deserted office and called out, "Is anybody here?" From somewhere in the back, a grease-stained, potbellied, red-nosed man, no more than five feet, three inches tall, shuffled out.

After the trucker explained the problem, the mechanic's watery blue eyes lit up. "Well, this calls for a road trip!" he said as he swung into action.

While Margie and Steve concluded their grateful thanks to the trucker, the little man phoned and woke up his nephew.

Nephew's displeasure rang through the phone wires as he ranted and raved loud enough for everyone in the small office to hear. "Hit's bad nuff you woke us, Uncle, when ah finally got me a date with Mary Sue. Now you want me to get myself down there?" Angry words were exchanged, but agreement was finally reached. While waiting for his nephew, the mechanic scurried around piling chains and ropes, wrenches and jacks—anything that might be helpful—into the back of his tow truck. The minute Nephew arrived, his uncle threw the keys at him and shouted out instructions to watch the shop.

As they headed toward their abandoned rig, Margie asked, "Why are we taking this road? It doesn't look like the way we came here."

"Well, young 'un, the sheriff in these here parts don't like me one bit. Ah reckon he's had it in for me since high school. We wuz both on our school's football team—real rivals, real enemies, right? Ole Charlie thought he had hisself a ticket to college, 'cause he could throw and ketch that li'l ball easier than pitchin' a hissy fit. Well, it wuz homecoming—theirs, not ours—and Ole Charlie struttin' and prancin' up and down that field like he owned it. He caught that pig's skin one time too many, and Ah tackled him real good. Reckon you could hear his knee bone crackin' all the way up in the top row. Ole Charlie never went to no college after that. And he sho do hold hisself a grudge. He hassle me ever' chance he gets—can't go nowhere on the roads, but there he be, hassle, hassle, hassle. So Ah know roads he don't and better we don't see his ugly face."

Margie and Steve looked at his small frame as they listened to his story, but figured worrying about his truthfulness wasn't going to help much at this point. Besides, he soon gave them something new to be concerned about. "People 'round here love to hunt. Can't find no bear, no deer, they'll find sumthin'. You say you got horses in that there van? Sure hope they's still there."

Steve and Margie exchanged *I-don't-believe-this!* looks. They glanced at their watches, noted the time of 2 A.M., and prayed their way out of this predicament. As they pulled up to the stranded truck and van, they heard the horses nickering a welcome. While they checked out and reassured the animals, Uncle assessed the damage."Yep, yo're gonna need a new axle. This here one done welded to the wheel."

Steve clenched his fists by his side. "And where in the hell are we supposed to get an axle?"

"In Roanoke for that, Ah reckon. Only take a couple of days."

"We don't have a couple of days! Come on, man, there must be something we can do. If we suspend this axle, we'll still have three good wheels on the trailer. What if we tied it up in any way possible? The truck's axles are good and it can still drive!"

Uncle scratched his head while he thought this over. "Okay, I'll jack up the axle and take off the tire." Steve swung into action. He wrapped first a chain, then some of the lead shanks from the trailer, around the axle and trailer frame. Uncle lowered the jack a little, then kicked it from under the trailer. The axle stayed suspended in the air.

They thanked Uncle profusely, paid him gladly, and proceeded slowly. At first they drove at a snail's pace, but gradually Steve's confidence returned and they picked up speed. Into the sunrise and out of the mountains, they headed once again for Roanoke.

"Margie, judging from your phone calls, you sure are involved with a lot of horse owners."

She mentioned a few names we recognized: Alan Chesler, Frances Snodgrass, Cristina Schlusemeyer. "I'll always save time for them. They gave me a chance when I was first starting out. But you're right, I am riding quite a few horses right now." Little did we realize exactly how many equaled "quite a few."

After several years of Margie's assuming full and final responsibility for every facet of her horse business, she was very happy to have Spank Deemer join the team. "Mom, Dad, wait till you meet Spank! He's had so much experience with show jumping both as a horse trainer and as a stable manager. And did I tell you about his many years as a football coach? He's really used to handling a wide variety of people."

We felt vast relief when her new manager proved himself capable and caring, both with the horses and with their owners. Furthermore, he adapted well to the job's frenetic schedule with his steady, easygoing assurance. Margie's cheering fans found it comforting to see Spank's trim form rushing to her aid or assistance both before and after her turn in the ring. Easy to identify because of his startling-white hair, the "Silver Fox" became a wonderful partner for more than two decades.

Margie's social life required attention also. Although she dated many fine young men, we and her friends were very partial to her transportation partner, who was now a full-time veterinarian. Steve approached his work and his play with the same level of intensity as our daughter. Not only did they share a passion for horses, but each respected the role the other performed

Two people who made life a lot easier for Margie: Kim Tudor, president of Sports-Mart, Ltd. and activities director for Stadium Jumping, and John "Spank" Deemer, Margie's right hand for two decades. Photographer: *Cheryl Bender* ©

with these gentle giants as well. He lovingly treated his four-legged patients with all the skills at his command and grieved when he could not save them from complications. Our daughter trusted his judgment completely.

When he arrived at our house to pick up Margie for an evening's entertainment, he waited more or less patiently. While she concluded a phone conversation with a client, he talked to us. Later either Irv or I commented, "Margie, Steve isn't happy with your being on the phone so much."

"I try to make it short. This is the way I earn a living. I have to be available when the clients are concerned about their horses. Steve should understand. Some of our dates end up with him taking care of a horse with colic." The more time we spent with him, the more we admired his steadiness, his values, and his positive attitude. There was just one problem. Where was this relationship headed?

Her friend Sherri could not hide her concern and expressed the worry all of us felt. "Marge, I don't understand what's happening. You and Steve have been dating for three years now. You both enjoy everything you do together. What's going on?"

From college, Nancy Unger called to say how much she had enjoyed spending the winter break in Miami. "You two are so perfect together. Do you have anything you want to tell me?"

Margie's answer to her friends was always the same. "We're both so busy trying to build our careers. It's awfully hard to plan anything else right now."

They parted as friends. Margie returned his investment in the transportation venture. Steve even visited me when I was recovering from surgery. We spoke about many things *except* for his plans to move to Texas, where he would start his large-animal veterinarian practice. I wished him good luck, but felt infinite sadness at his and Margie's decision to part.

CHAPTER NINE

Enter Daydream

"MOM, YOU HAVE A BIRTHDAY COMING UP SOON. What would you like?"

"You really want to give me something I would appreciate more than anything else I can think of?"

Margie looked at me questioningly. "Ye-e-s?"

"Well, what I really want more than any tangible gift is an hour of your time—one whole hour completely uninterrupted, no calls from friends or clients, our very own yours-and-mine time-to-talk hour."

"What did you want to talk about?"

"When we have the hour, I'll tell you."

More than six months would pass before I received my belated birthday present. I wasted not a minute.

"Margie, I've loved having you for a daughter. Right from day one, you have brought so much happiness to your father and me, to your brothers, except for—maybe—the only times we had difficulty with raising you."

She finished the thought for me, "When we were in elementary school together."

"That's right. You sure were a mischievous little girl. That time—and from the time you turned twenty to right now at twenty-three."

A look of shock flashed across her expressive face. "I *really* don't understand. I'm on the road 80 percent of the year. I'm not even *here* most of the time."

"I think you've got it! Margie, do you ever plan on settling down? How are you going to meet decent men? Don't you eventually want a husband? Children?"

"Mom, please remember I'm *not* you. You were happy to get married at eighteen, have children early, and then go back to teaching. I don't plan to get married until I'm much older."

"But, honey, how can you even meet anyone with the life you lead? You're on the road so much, and you don't spend enough time in each place to even begin a relationship."

"Mom, I have plenty of dates, and I've had quite a few proposals."

"But what do you know about them? What kind of backgrounds do they have? That vet you dated up north didn't sound too stable to me—building a shrine made up of your newspaper clippings!"

"Mom, he scared me, too! I didn't date him long, only once or twice, and I made sure we stayed in large groups."

"Margie, what happened between you and Steve? The two of you obviously cared for each other deeply, yet—after more than three years—you split up."

"I *did* care for Steve and, if I don't ever meet anyone like him, I may never marry. Not everybody feels the same as you."

"Perhaps not. I just want you to be happy. I'd like you to have the warmth and security of family even when you're older and no longer able to work as hard as you do now. Why *are* you working such long hours anyway?"

"Mom, you just don't understand. The professionals are telling me I'm too little for the large horses—that I'll never be able to control them. I *know* I can do it. I'll just have to keep showing them I can. When some of the owners have a horse the other riders don't want to show, they're willing to take a chance on me. One of these days, I'll prove I can be as good as the best."

We saw Margie's goals from different viewpoints, but I used every second of my hour and thanked her for the gift.

The extensive travels continued. "Hi, Mom. Hi, Dad."

"Where are you calling from, honey?"

1983   The "little Goldstein girl" did a lot of autographing in Attitash.

"I'm in Attitash, New Hampshire. You'd love it. The people are so nice, and the arena sits in the middle of the mountains. Everywhere you look you can see the trees with their bright colors and the hills in the background."

"We'll keep it in mind. How's the show going?"

Margie laughed. "Well, there are quite a few older Jewish tourists in this area. Evidently they've read about me in the local paper, because they'll stop to ask where the little Goldstein girl is. The other riders tease me with, 'Margie, your people are looking for you.' Anyway, I won a first, a third, and a fourth in the Grand Prix. This place seems to be lucky for me."

"You did rather well in New York last week also."

"New York was fun for other reasons as well. Did I tell you I saw both Andrea and Bobbi when I was there? In fact, Bobbi was my chaperone."

"How did that happen?"

"When she came to visit me at the hotel, I had a date with a guy named Lou. Since we didn't know each other that well, I told Bobbi she had to come along—I needed her."

61

"Honey, you may be a daredevil in the ring, but we're sure glad you're cautious about some things. Give Bobbi and Andrea our best the next time you see them."

"I certainly will. Dad, did you receive the checks I mailed you for deposit?"

"Yes, and we see that you're really turning your hobby into a paying proposition. Good for you!"

Except when she was on the circuit, Margie lived at home, and her bank account was growing. Not only was she earning money from lessons, from commissions when she brokered horse sales, and from fees for riding for many owners, but she received a percentage of the purse when she and a horse won as well.

Margie rode and rode and rode. Whatever was offered to her, she showed.

"Margie, my horse is acting up. I've already paid the entry fee. Can you ride him for me?"

1984   J. Buffet could drop a leg badly if you let him fall on his forehand or get too close to a fence, but balanced properly, he was a good jumper and very kind. He stayed in the top three in the country as a first-year horse, second-year horse, and two years as a regular working hunter. Photographer: *Judith S. Buck* ©

1984 When Margie started showing Sneak Preview in green hunters, she tended to jump past her arc (touching down farther from the jump than she took off) and to slap out over the jumps. To improve her jumping style, she worked on gymnastics with rails nine feet in front of the jump and nine feet in back. This helped her keep her arc centered and prevented her from slapping out over the fence. The improved jumping style made her one of the most successful hunters in the country. Photographer: *Judith S. Buck* ©

"Margie, I'd like to move up to a more competitive horse. Can you ride and win on my present horse so we can sell him?"

We'd go to a horse show and never be able to talk to her. After watching a show-jumping event, we'd head for the barns. "Where is she?"

"Oh, she's in the junior arena coaching one of her pupils." Or "Well, she's over in the hunter ring with one of the new horses."

She rode and rode and rode. Difficult horses. Horses with potential. Horses who needed coddling. Horses who needed firmness. Thirty, forty, occasionally sixty horses a day. Sometimes her legs were bloody from all the rubbing and chafing.

Finally, in 1986, two good hunters provided her with national attention. J. Buffet, a large gray horse, won many blue ribbons. Sneak Preview, a smaller 15.3-hand chestnut, won championship tricolors at every show she entered that year except one, in which she won Reserve Champion. When

Margie first started showing Sneak Preview, the mare tended to jump past her arc and slap out over the jumps. To improve her style, as Margie told us, "We use gymnastics and other exercises. By placing rails on the ground nine feet in front of the jump and nine feet behind it, we get her to keep her arc in the center of the fences. That way, we keep her from slapping out also."

The mare became national champion as a second-year green hunter, and was sold for the highest price paid for a hunter up to that time, resulting in Margie's attracting the attention of several friends and other people connected to horses in various ways.

1986   Puck W., a large Hanovarian, was known as an extremely strong and difficult horse. When he saw the jump, he would grab the bit and run at it, landing completely out of control. Margie spent many hours of slow and patient work doing figure eights in front of the fence, trotting and cantering until he learned to relax and not anticipate jumping. Additionally, he would jump into a line and not take the correct number of strides. Margie made him take seven strides instead of six, so he learned to land and wait for the rider's instructions rather than rush the fence. In flatwork and gymnastics practice, she avoided interfering with his mouth, letting the striding, placement poles, and guide rails tell him what to do and how to do it. Credit: *author's collection*

* * *

Dr. Engle called long distance. "Hey, old friend, I've been treating a horse you really ought to try out. Think you can squeeze in a trip to Texas?" Margie hesitated. Steve continued, "I think he's a beauty. He's extremely high-spirited and athletic. He moves easily and likes to jump over anything in his path. This may be the horse who'll give you a shot at the big time."

"Steve, when you say he's high-spirited and will jump over everything, are you comparing him to Puck?"

"No, Puck isn't just spirited, he's crazy! Margie, it's time you stopped riding such wild horses. Remember when you finished the course and he continued galloping—right next to the stands and over the lady in the golf cart?"

"How could I forget? But that's not why you called. Tell me more about your find."

"He's a large dapple-gray—almost white—Hanovarian gelding, five years old, and stands 17.1 hands high. When I told the owner, Max Fanninger, about you, he said you were probably too small to be able to control Daydream. Then he saw you riding Puck in Culpeper, Virginia, and I didn't have to sell him anymore. He said if you're tough enough and hungry enough to ride *that* horse, you'd have no trouble with his."

For Margie and Daydream, it was love at first sight. Daydream had complete trust in her and would do anything she asked. She was thrilled with his natural scope, jumping power, and athleticism. He was a little slow with his front end, but the gymnastics and exercises they practiced made him sharper, quicker, and less likely to hit fences with his forelegs. The exercises included no strides or bounces, trotting to small verticals two and a half to three feet high and placed nine or ten feet apart, and cantering in-and-outs (vertical to oxer, set between twenty and twenty-two feet apart). Each time they worked out, Margie stroked and brushed him. "You *are* a beauty! Together we just may make it after all."

Margie pushed Daydream almost as hard as she pushed herself. Gradually, throughout 1986, we heard about a win here, a win there, another one at a different horse show. "Mom, Dad, I've got enough points to go to the big Madison Square Garden show!"

"Wonderful!"

Daydream's natural scope, jumping power, and athleticism made him easy to ride. Margie felt his front end was slow, so she used no strides or bounces and low verticals between two and a half and three feet, set nine to ten feet apart. "We also trotted him and practiced in-and-outs (vertical to an oxer) set between twenty and twenty-two feet apart, then cantered him to get quicker and sharper with the front end."
Photography: *Pennington Galleries*

But it wasn't wonderful. A couple of weeks later, Margie's dispirited voice told us that she was in New York. She had the points to qualify as one of the four official United States Equestrian Team (USET) riders in the Nation's Cup, but somehow someone else had been named the team representative.

"Margie, that's so unfair. Are you going to fight it?"

"I could win the battle and lose the war. I'm just going to try harder. Daydream and I are here, and we'll show on our own."

I talked to a friend of Margie's and remarked how stoic she was. The answer came quickly. "She's more vulnerable than she will let you know. I saw her after she got the news about not being named to the team, and she went behind a wall where she thought no one could see her. When I heard her crying, I thought maybe it was good to let it out, and I never let her know I saw her."

Irv and I, with great difficulty, said nothing also. For Margie, who rode Daydream and Spindletop USA, the outcome couldn't have been more satisfying. When the show ended, Margie, in her first-time appearance at Madison Square Garden, earned the title Leading Open Jumper Rider, 1986.

When she called us in the middle of the next year's fall circuit, we could hear the excitement in her voice. "Margie, slow down. What did you say?"

She enunciated with great precision, "Mom, Dad, I've qualified for all three international competitions. That means I'm now an official USET member. We'll be showing in Washington, at Madison Square Garden, and in Toronto, *Canada*! Is there any chance you can come?"

Both of us groaned. "With our work schedules, it's impossible," Irv said. "You don't know it yet, but Mom finally has her own school."

"Yes," I added. "It only took me five years as an assistant principal, a year of interning as a principal, three years of interviews, and twenty times

The costume classes at Madison Square Garden in 1986 added a light approach. Fantastique, a big-boned German-bred gelding, had a stubborn attitude about water jumps, so he needed constant repetition jumping liverpools and others until it became automatic. Photography: *Pennington Galleries*

Spindletop USA, a Belgian Warmblood, had a tendency to take advantage of any situation. He needed a very assertive ride in the schooling area to make him respect a rider. Margie rode Spindletop USA and Daydream to earn Champion Open Speed Rider 1986 at Madison Square Garden. Photographer: *Randy Myers*

of making the finals for it to happen. The promotion was worth waiting for, but this first year will be especially busy. Will the shows be televised?" The truth was that it was far easier on our nerves to see the delayed broadcast when we knew that Margie was safe.

The TV camera faithfully captured the excitement of Washington's Puissance, or high-jumping, competition. The arena was empty with the exception of two jumps. The announcer explained, "Within each round, the eight horse–rider combinations will use the smaller hurdle to practice, then attempt to clear the high jump. If any portion is knocked down, the pair is eliminated. Another row of Styrofoam 'brick' blocks will be added for the next round, and each successful rider will be allowed to continue."

The audience alternately cheered or groaned as they watched the number of riders dwindle. At last only one remained. As Margie attempted to jump seven feet, seven and three-quarters inches to tie the world's indoor record for height during a Puissance performance, voices rang out, "Go, Margie. Come on, Daydream." The tension mounted. As Daydream pushed upward, every muscle in his body seemed to stretch. A moment later, the announcer told the crowd, "They did it! They did it! Ladies and gentlemen, you've seen a world record tonight."

While the spectators still stood applauding this accomplishment, Margie was asked whether she and Daydream would try for a *new* world record. The crowd fell silent. Margie knew Daydream would follow her lead. She hesitated, yet he had felt strong and was breathing evenly. She nodded. The crowd roared its approval. The obstacles were placed higher until the formidable wall now measured seven feet, eight and three-quarters inches.

At the 1986 Washington International, Margie and Daydream won the Puissance event. Never was the rapport between horse and rider more evident. Basically, the horse must jump a blank wall with no assurance of what is on the other side.
Photographer: *Al Cook Photography*

Daydream leaped upward, straining every muscle in his body. His back leg barely touched one of the bricks, and it fell to the ground. He landed with such force on his front legs that he tripped. The offstride landing sent Margie sailing over his head. I gasped, then rose from the couch, walked over to Margie, and hugged her as hard as I could. "Thank God, you're here and unharmed. I would *never* be able to watch that in person!"

The film that followed clearly showed an unharmed Daydream desperately trying to avoid stepping on the fallen rider. The camera panned in so close, we saw his foot next to Margie's neck. Spank had rushed to check on Margie, helped her to her feet, and the two figures walked out of the arena: one steadily, the other badly shaken. When we made that comment to her, she retorted, "Yeah, Spank does look rather shaken, doesn't he?" Margie was able to joke, but no matter how many times ESPN replayed this sequence, we saw little except Daydream's foot next to our daughter's neck.

"Hi, Mom and Dad. I sure wish you could have been here. Toronto really rolled out the welcome mat, and even though it's cold and windy outside, we hardly feel it. Our hotel is in the center of town, and all the buildings and stores are interlinked with underground tunnels. You'd love it."

"You're right. We thoroughtly enjoyed Toronto when we were there a few years ago. But tell us, how are you feeling? How are the classes going?"

"I can't believe how the Canadians love their show jumpers! Ian Millar, remember? I told you he won the World Cup, not once—but twice! Anyway, he's a national hero. They call him Captain Canada, and the news media follow him wherever he goes. The royal family sends a personal representative from Great Britain for their international shows, and the stands are filled for all the events. There are twenty thousand eager fans for almost every class. For the evening classes, everyone wears long gowns and tuxedos."

"Sounds mighty exciting. What about the high-jumping class—how did you and Daydream do?"

"Oh, you mean the Puissance?" Margie asked and then described her experience.

On the scheduled night, she and Daydream waited in the designated area, a small schooling arena where the riders could warm up the horses over *small* jumps—from three feet up to four feet, nine inches. The Puissance competition is so difficult for the horse and his slender legs that a concerned rider will never add to that strain with larger fences. Because success in this class is based not just on talent alone but also on complete trust between partners, only a small number of rider–horse combinations competed.

As Margie and Daydream entered the arena, soared over the practice fence, and cantered toward the high jump, the crowd fell silent. Six feet, five inches jumped and cleared smoothly. Success. The wall was raised. And raised again. Soon additional wooden "bricks" brought the wall to seven feet. Margie felt Daydream's heart beat faster. Once again, they cleared the high jump. Margie listened to the sound of Daydream's loud breathing. "Okay, good buddy, you're doing fine. Let's go for it." The murmur in the crowd buzzed through the stadium as they watched the height of the fence soar upward.

At seven feet, four inches, the wall looked like the side of a building. All Margie heard was the sound of her own heart pumping blood and adrenaline through every inch of her body. Would Daydream follow her guidance? As Margie and Daydream cleared the wall, the murmur of the crowd thundered to a pulsating roar. The thrill of victory surged through her being as she hugged her scopey steed.

Later that evening, Margie—still in her riding clothes—was introduced to an elegantly clad duchess from Great Britain. Her silver-gray hair was adorned with a glittering diamond tiara, and a satin sash across her impressive ball gown displayed a variety of jeweled medals. Her assured and regal voice rang out, "I say, are you the little girl who won the Puissance earlier?" Margie acknowledged the recognition.

The duchess leaned over, tapped Margie's riding breeches with her cane, and asked with great dignity, "Young lady, do you have *balls* down there?"

Overhearing the conversation, Frank Chapot, who had been in six consecutive Olympic Games and who was now serving as the team's chef d'équipe, inquired, "Did I hear what I thought I heard? What did you answer?"

Margie shook her head and blinked her eyes. "For the first time in my life, I was speechless!" Show jumping did have its surprises.

Among the season's happy surprises and delights, the Puissance trophy in Washington was retired in honor of Daydream and Margie's winning performances three years in a row. In addition, this Terrific Twosome were the only horse-and-rider combination to win all three Puissance Classes in one year during the International Indoor Circuit.

Then too, their outstanding wins in specific qualifying Grand Prix events earned them a spot for their first appearance in World Cup competition in Göteborg, Sweden, in 1988.

"Isn't it exciting? We have a wonderful team. USET will pay for all our expenses—bringing the horses over by plane, the hotel where we're staying. I can't believe I'm going to Europe!"

Margie's elation was short-lived. Her weekly phone call home began in a low, dispirited voice: "Mom, Dad, one of the riders has offered to buy Daydream from Max at a price he doesn't feel he can refuse. It looks as if I won't be going to Sweden after all."

"Oh, no. Why can't Max sell him *after* the World Cup?"

"The talk is that if I have no horse to ride, the next ranked rider will have an opportunity to move up and become our U.S. representative. I can't believe this is happening."

"Mighty Mite, even you can't jump without a horse! This is much too important to your career. What if we're able to raise the money?"

Within the next month, Margie's dad, using his knowledge as a certified public accountant plus the services of a lawyer, had a proposal ready. The legal document looked impressive. It included pictures and outlined the financial requirements for owning shares in Daydream, Inc. Margie, her dad, and I approached any and all likely candidates and compared results. "Any luck yet?"

"No, not a nibble. Unfortunately, a recent law has minimized the tax advantages in such a venture, and people aren't anxious to gamble. They want their money to work for them."

As the weeks went by and no shares were sold, we finally admitted defeat in that effort. An SOS went out to all the family, telling about the projected sale of Daydream and how Margie would not be able to go to the World Cup without him. "How would you like to own a portion of a horse?

You can have the end that eats," we asked. Uncle Wally and Aunt Dee (Irv's sister) Berman, Uncle Eddie (my brother) and Aunt Nancy Pastroff, her father and I, as well as Margie herself, pooled our resources and reached the owner's asking price. Each of us jokingly identified the portion of Daydream we now claimed financially. For the first time in her life, Margie owned a horse—even if it was only *part* ownership!

Soon Margie's "stable" expanded even farther. One evening after a busy Houston horse show, Margie was catching up with her laundry. As luck would have it, right near the Laundromat was a pet store. As Margie browsed through the aisles, one particularly appealing little dachshund caught her eye.

Oscar became Margie's constant companion, traveling by her side, adapting to her nomadic lifestyle, and playing with the horses while he waited for her to return from the field. Photographer: *Judith S. Buck* ©

Every time she came back from checking her clothes—as Margie later told everyone—"He just seemed to talk to me." From that moment on, Oscar Meyer and Margie became inseparable. He followed her wherever she went, traveled to most of the horse shows, and—somehow or other—managed to avoid being trampled as he played between and under his horse friends.

Oscar appealed to many of Margie's interviewers, who found it easy to find her stables when they spotted his familiar low-slung form darting in and out of the backstage showgrounds.

"Margie, you're developing quite a reputation as a 'catch rider.' Why is this?" asked one reporter.

"I think I've always been a catch rider. I'll ride any horse at any time, even if someone offers that horse at the last minute. Naturally, I prefer to

Margie had no difficulty training the smallest member of her troupe.
Photographer: *Judith S. Buck* ©

know a horse before I go into the ring, but I haven't always had that luxury."

Luxury? Margie rode as many as sixty-five rounds in one day! The years of riding the most difficult horses "anytime, anyplace" were now paying off. Margie had developed a horse sense, and the horses responded with their best effort. If clients owned large, slightly rebellious horses, they thought of her and her ability to capitalize on the animals' strengths. The horses trusted her, as she did them. Margie coaxed the best from them all, employing what some announcers called the "Goldstein Growl," verbal encouragement that spurred many a reluctant mare or stallion to make that extra effort.

CHAPTER TEN

The Big Push

ALONG WITH RECOGNITION CAME SUPPORT FROM FANS. We enjoyed reading their letters as much as our daughter did. We were not surprised when Margie heard from many children, but we reacted with astonishment that so many adults wrote to her. Young adults often spoke glowingly about how gutsy she was or thanked her for words of advice she gave when they saw her at shows or wrote to her. Older individuals confided personal experiences, even to tell her when they had lost a spouse or other loved one.

"Margie, this letter sounds as if you've written to her before," I commented one day.

"Oh, I always answer the mail I receive."

"When on earth do you find the time?"

"I have to spend so much time in airports or airplanes. That's when I take care of my correspondence and—*other paperwork*," she answered, emphasizing the last two words for the benefit of her father.

"And well you should" came the unruffled reply.

Although fans and owners accepted Margie well, her dad and I wondered about her reception from other riders. This question was answered for us in Tampa's Winter Circuit of 1989. After the evening events were over, we looked around the fairground for our daughter. We noticed a rather large crowd still in their riding outfits. As the laughter erupted from the group, we spotted a tiny figure in the center busy telling one joke after another. Who else? It was Margie—still the class clown who always left them laughing.

Behind the laughter was mutual respect. Show jumping is a sport in which the more the rider observes and listens to top horsemen and trainers, the more he or she learns. Even to this day, Margie still critiques the tapes of her performance and those of the other top equestrians.

"Great job, Margie! Think we'll be riding together in the World Cup?" encouraged Olympian and Pan Am champion Michael Matz, one of the riders Margie watched every time he mounted a horse.

Rodney Jenkins, the charming red-haired Virginian who was one of the best riders of the twentieth century with more than seventy Grand Prix wins to his credit, told Spank, "That's the toughest little girl I've ever seen. She could probably go b'ar [bear] hunting with a switch."

"I liked your interview, little one," noted Mark Leone, one of three brothers who, as Team Leone, had brought an added interest to equestrian sports.

"Well done, old friend." Margie turned around at the sound of a familiar voice. The surprised look on her face brought a bemused smile to his.

"Steve, what are you doing here in Palm Beach?"

"It's a long, sad story, and I really don't want to talk about it. For your information, I no longer live in Texas. I've moved back to North Miami. I'm working at the track, taking care of their horses, and doing extra work at the horse shows."

Margie took a long look at his gaunt frame and unhappy eyes and decided no further questions were necessary. "Steve, am I glad to see you! Come take a look at Daydream. He's everything you said he would be." Both of them continued their conversation as if there had not been a four-year interruption.

"Where are you calling from, Marge? Your mail is piling up. Where will you be during the next two weeks?"

Keeping up with Margie's travels was becoming increasingly difficult. One of the horse magazines found her itinerary so interesting that it printed a map of the United States and traced the route that Margie had covered in one year. This whirlwind coverage, as well as the many horses she was showing, led to several unusual records: "Only Rider to Win Grand Prixes in Two Cities in a Twenty-Four-Hour Period," "Only Rider to Place First, Second, and Third in One Grand Prix," "Only Rider to Place Four Horses in One Grand Prix," and "Only Rider to Place First Through Fifth in a Single Grand Prix," plus "Most Wins [Thirteen] for a Rider in One Season."

With so many wins, Margie began to overtake Jeffrey Welles for the coveted AGA Rider of the Year 1989. This recognition is based on the number of points earned at AGA weekly competitions. For example, the first-place rider, who receives 30 percent of the announced winnings, might win a purse of $30,000 in a $100,000 class; the second-place rider receives 22 percent, or $22,000; and so on down the line, until the final rider to be placed (number ten through twelve, depending on the total purse) might win $1,000. The money goes to the horse's owner, but the rider earns a percentage of the winnings plus one computer point for every $1,000 won and one point for every clear round.

Jeff teased Margie as her points accumulated: "So you're going to make it hard for me, huh? I guess I'll just have to win big in the next class."

She retorted with the same easy comraderie, "You didn't think I'd let you off easy, Jeff. I'm going to make you really work for every point you earn."

The two riders were so close that the final competition of the year would decide who would be that year's champion. Neither rider had to *win* the final AGA Grand Prix in Tampa. One simply had to have a better score than the other.

We sat in the Tampa stands surrounded by friends and fans of Margie's who'd driven or flown from Miami just to be there for her biggest challenge to date.

Margie rode before Jeff, because he was slightly ahead of her going into the competition. She gave Daydream a final hug, and the two athletes entered the arena. Daydream bolted slightly at the noise that rose from the spectators. Margie quickly brought him under control and began the course. They seemed to glide across the jumps. Suddenly one of the planks fell to the ground, along with Margie's hopes and dreams.

Jeff followed. If he rode a perfect round, the crown was his. As he circled the field, he approached each hurdle with caution. He was wise to be

In 1989, Margie won her first AGA Rider of the Year Award and received a great "trophy." Photographer: *Tish Quirk*

so careful. The friends and family of each rider gasped. A rail was down. Who was the winner? With both of them tied in this round, the one with the faster time would receive the higher score in the rankings. The judges checked the time and checked again. By only seconds, Margie had become the 1989 AGA Rider of the Year. Cadillac, the sponsor, handed her the keys to her new Cadillac Allante, and Margie took her "victory gallop" around the field, waving happily to one and all.

At the gala celebration that evening, we met many of the owners for whom Margie rode. Max Fanninger, who had spent his youth in Austria but was now an American citizen, charmed us with his proper European manners and accent, as well as his knowledge of horses.

Jacob Friedus had been in New York real estate, but was now retired. In his younger days, he had ridden and competed in horse shows, and his knowledge was extensive. We recognized his name from the many phone calls he made to our daughter. In his day, riding was not so sophisticated, so he thought the care Margie provided her horses was pampering. I had watched her face as he argued with her, "Leg wraps? Blankets? Are you trying to spoil my horses?" Still, they were his babies, and, even though he couldn't travel to many shows, because of his daily calls to Margie and the show's personnel he knew everything that happened.

Winning her first national championship opened up even more opportunities. Several clients, who trusted her judgment totally, sent her to Europe to purchase horses whom she felt had promise.

When she returned, we asked, "How was your first trip to Europe, honey?" She gave us the names of several horses and the people she had purchased them for. "Great! Hopefully, they'll fulfill your expectations. What sights did you see?"

"Well, we had such a rushed trip that I saw only horse barns. Beautiful barns, especially the ones in Germany. I couldn't get over how clean they were and how elaborately they were built! They served us lunch in one of the barns, and it was like dining in an elegant hotel."

"Were you able to see anything else?"

"No. Patti Harnois—my friend from Massachusetts—Max, and I drove from one country to another, one barn to another. I had to show horses the next day after we flew home."

"Oh, Margie, you're the only one I know who goes to Europe and sees only barns—what a shame!"

The next time we saw Patti, we commiserated with her about their breakneck trip across the Continent. "You know your daughter. Almost everything she does is fast. But she's slow and patient with the horses once she works with them. She really gets into their heads with the time she takes with them, her kindness, and her knowledge of their individual traits. They'll do anything for her."

When other sports-minded owners offered her a chance at horses who already had victories in lesser classes, she welcomed the opportunity. Margie was all set to ride one stallion that showed enormous potential. Two days prior to the scheduled Sunday event, she received a call.

The voice on the phone was low and emotionless, but the words chilled her: "Margie, if you ride this horse, you'll have an accident."

She was sure she had heard incorrectly. "What did you say?" The caller repeated his message in the same ominous tone.

"Who is this? Why are you threatening me?"

"You don't have to know who this is. The horse's owner owes one of the van companies money and we won't let any of his horses show until he pays us."

"I'll call the police. Your problem is not with me. I've never even shown any of his horses."

"You can call anyone you want. If you ride his horse, you'll be hurt or we'll hurt one of the horses. If it doesn't happen Sunday, it'll happen another day. You'll always have to expect us."

We watched the concern in our daughter's face, and even though we could only hear her end of the conversation, we knew something was not right. "What's going on? That did not sound good."

She replied in an incredulous voice, "I can't believe they're threatening me. I've never been on the horse. I've never had dealings with the horse owner. Why are they after me because the owner owes money to a horse van company?"

The menacing phone call had accomplished what the unknown terrorist had desired. I looked at Irv's worried face and wondered if it reflected the raw concern I felt in every fiber of my body. "Margie, you don't intend to ride the horse, do you?"

"I don't see how I possibly can under these circumstances."

When she talked to the owner, explaining her reasons for turning down his horse, he agreed that he would pay his long-owed debts. "You'll start with a clean slate," he said. "I've watched you ride and I really want you to show my horse. What would it take to make that happen?"

Margie responded, "I don't ever want to be in a position like this again. Several of the riders told me that they've shown your horses and never been paid. The same thing with the blacksmiths. The stall owners say you're slow in paying them, too. I'll only ride your horse if you let me handle the finances. Your horse is wonderful. Once you're paid up to date, I'll pay the future expenses—entry fees, stall rentals, blacksmiths, and feed—and you'll repay me from the horses' winnings."

It took a full year before her gamble paid off. All of the owner's bills were paid on time by Margie. When his horses won, she took out her percentage of the winnings, paid off any bills that were due, and sent him the remainder.

When the owner complained about having to wait for his share, Margie retorted, "Tell me what bank will give you an interest-free loan for a year!" He was silenced, but only temporarily. Margie sold one of his horses a few weeks later, and he was back on the attack. "That was an easy sale. You can have exactly half of your commission."

"I don't believe you understand," Margie told him. "I'm following the guidelines—no more, no less. You owe me a full commission."

"That depends of how you look at it. Take half. It's more than you would have had before the horse was sold."

"As I said, I don't think you realize what is involved. I've trained the horse and won ribbons with him. This increases his value. I've had to schedule viewings and fly back to show him. All of this takes time."

"You don't have to tell me," the owner insisted. "I've had a lot of experience. You're just getting started. You need to take anything you can get. Take half."

On and on they went. After two hours, Margie said, "I can't take this constant haggling. You want your horses back, I'll ship them back—COD."

"Fine. You want to lose your commission, that's okay with me."

The next day, the owner was back on the phone. "Okay, you don't have to send the horses here. Take your full commission."

"You mean you kept me on the phone two hours and you were ready to concede the whole time!"

"Well, you can't blame me for trying," he said.

The next time we saw our daughter, she brought us up to date on her dealings with this man who was so wealthy, but so incapable of paying his debts. I answered, "What a penny-pincher! You must be totally frustrated."

"I sure wish I could tell him where to go, but did you know that even the government can't seem to do that? I've been reading in the paper that he has already been in jail for nonpayment of taxes. So at least I've been paid, even if I have to fight for every dollar due."

"You'll be doing more than reading the paper soon," I told her. "It seems Uncle Sam is determined to get what is due also. Dad was contacted by the IRS, and they're increasing their pursuit of your client. The agent said they've already invested twenty years and they want closure. They're requiring a copy of every single financial dealing you've ever had with him. Fortunately, with a little prodding from your father, all your records are complete!"

A stunned taxpayer replied, "Dad, it may have taken me a while, but I'm so glad you forced your advice upon me. I hate the extra time I have to spend keeping good records, but I'm sure relieved I don't have to look over *my* shoulder!"

In March 1990, Margie rode Roman Delight, a two-thousand-pound stallion, in the Tampa preliminaries. Everything was going well until we received an unexpected call. "Margie, you sound terrible. What's happened?"

"Mom, Dad, please don't worry. I've been to the best sports doctors here in Tampa. My left leg is in a plaster cast."

"Oh, no! No! Why? What happened?"

We could hear Margie take a deep breath. "The horse was trying so hard, but the footing was deep. As we turned a corner, he slipped, landed on his side with my foot—under his full weight—caught between the saddle and metal stirrup. The X-rays show that all the small bones in that foot and ankle are crushed."

"Margie, what is the prognosis?"

She paused, but knew that we would find out one way or another. "They tell me that I'll never walk normally again and—because of the nerve damage—they question whether I'll ever ride again."

Margie's wins had qualified her for a long-held dream, the American International, which was a week away. Laden down with a plaster cast, she attempted to compete. As she sat on the horse, spasms of pain contorted her body. The absolute agony prevented her from continuing. She was devastated. In ten weeks, she tried again using a specially constructed boot on the painful, raw-nerved foot.

"Honey, how are you doing? We're quite concerned about your using only one stirrup while you're showing. Doesn't that throw you off balance?"

"Well, it sure doesn't help. But would you believe I placed in the top three in my first two Grand Prix since returning? One of the horses I'm now riding is called Saluut II. Remember you met his owner, Jacob Friedus, in Tampa? He looks a lot like Daydream—also dapple gray. He's a

Dutch-bred stallion and stands 16.2 hands tall. More importantly, he's a real champion. He has so much heart and he's so-o-o careful. Anything I ask of him he does! Saluut is the finest horse I ever rode!"

Despite her pain and inability to feel the horse's reactions—or perhaps *because* of this—Margie was more determined than ever. She had her cast painted black to look like a boot, trying to hide her infirmity, though at this point, the fans knew all about her condition. She could not walk around the fairground where the horse show was, so she used golf carts to get from one ring to another. But put her on a horse and that was another story! Even with so much time lost because of her injury, she managed to end the 1990 year in the top ten of the final standings.

The year 1991 bristled with activity. In his book *National to National: A Year on the Show Jumping Circuit*, David W. Hollis wrote about the events of that year. It began with a burst of patriotism in support of the U.S. fighters in the Persian Gulf. Course designer Steve Stephens featured red, white, and blue hurdles with large yellow ribbons tied on the jump standards. During the year, scandal broke out when a show-jumping horse was viciously attacked in an insurance scam. Also, one of the major riders sued the U.S. Equestrian Team. And of course, the intensity and expertise of the riders as they traveled and competed throughout the year kept readers captivated from one page to the next.

"Irv, I love this book. Not only is it extremely well written, but Margie has a chapter of her own—Little Lady on a Big Roll." I read and reread the accounts of our daughter's successful pursuits and creative air travel. I laughed as the author described Puck as a "moose in horse's clothing" and agreed with his description of Margie as starting out without the money to buy fancy, made horses or the connections to get them.

Still noticeably limping in that year following her injury, Margie rode to win six Grand Prix events, including the Attitash Equine Festival for the second year in a row. She also placed four horses in a single Grand Prix competition. She earned her way through qualifying competitions to become a member of several U.S. Equestrian Teams, won her second Rider of the Year Award, and was an odds-on favorite to compete for the United States in the Olympics.

The 1989 Rider of the Year Award had been close. The 1991 competition with Saluut and Daydream both available resulted in a hard-fought but easy win. With this second national award, *Sports Illustrated* featured Margie and her mounts in their only recognition to date of a show-jumping athlete.

"Margie, that was absolutely a terrific article about you in *Sports Illustrated*! They wrote about you and Saluut quite positively."

"They sure did. When people see Saluut's name on the license plate of my car, they honk at me and give me the *Okay* sign with their fingers."

"Well, that could be because Wellington is horse country and the Palm Beach people recognize his name. How's your new home there? Are you meeting many of your neighbors?"

In 1991, Saluut II, a 16.2-hand Dutch Holsteiner stallion, helped Margie win her second AGA Rider of the Year Award. Saluut made up in heart and carefulness for what he lacked in scope. Alert, anxious to please, fast in the jump-offs, he loved his job and quickly became one of Margie's favorite mounts. He still holds the record for most Grand Prix wins in a year. The only adjustment Margie made was in the height of his jump. "You always had to ride the back rail of the oxers and make sure he didn't overjump the height and not get across the width. She approached the jump with more pace to provide impulsion (energy from hind end, animation more forward)." Photographer: *Judith S. Buck* ©

"Oh, it's great place to live, and I love this area. I'm so glad to own a house up here rather than renting a place for three months of the circuit year."

With the second Rider of the Year Award came her second Cadillac. Her father and I congratulated her. "Margie, that's wonderful! Will they let you take the money instead of another car?"

"I didn't ask. I've arranged to trade in my first Cadillac for one of your choice. I didn't think you wanted a convertible, but they have many for you to select from."

"That's extremely generous of you, but we can't accept it."

"Why? Would you deny me that pleasure?"

When we saw how delighted our daughter was, we tried to accept her gracious gift in the same spirit.

We rejoiced in Margie's career accomplishments, but there always seemed to be a new worry around. "You're going to Europe *alone?*" or "What's going on with Steve? Are you dating anyone else?"

Margie's friends Sherri, Bobbi, and Nancy were all married at this point, and they, too, pressured Margie. "How many years are you and Steve going to date?" "Your body clock is ticking, old girl." "So what about the guy from New York who keeps calling you? And the one in Miami who wants to give you an engagement ring?"

We listened to our daughter's lament about her closest friends badgering her, but the reality was that Irv and I were very happy to have them voice our concerns.

Although she was still limping, Margie had recovered from her most serious injury to date. Winning two Rider of the Year Awards encouraged her toward pursuing her childhood dream of representing her country in the Olympic Games.

As soon as Irv and I heard Margie's voice, we anticipated bad news. She sounded low and dispirited on the phone. "Mom, Dad, you won't believe what happened. I'm in New York checking on Saluut. There's been a breeding accident, and Saluut's hind leg has been injured. We don't know if he can ever show again."

I heard a loud intake of air and realized it had come from me. "Oh, Margie, that's horrible. You must be terribly disappointed!"

Irv's voice sounded as barely in control as mine. "One of our friends *just* sent us an article about Saluut. He holds the record for Grand Prix wins in one year—nine—and the most AGA wins in one year—five. Is there any chance that you can enter the trials with Daydream?"

"I'll try. Daydream is a great horse, but not quite as consistent as Saluut."

Margie and Daydream entered the Olympic Trials but were unable to make the top four spots. Her disappointment in not representing her country in Barcelona was shared by family and friends. We, as well as Margie's aunt and uncle, canceled our reservations for Barcelona. As Margie joked with her old friend Steve Engle, "It only hurts when I laugh."

CHAPTER ELEVEN

Living Life to the Fullest

FOR THOSE WHO KNEW HER WELL, Margie and laughter became almost one. She told jokes with the best of them, and her "skits on horses" costume classes always were filled with good humor. Perhaps it was her smiling face that made her so approachable. Not only did she sign autographs for hours on end, but she continued to answer all her fans as well—young and old.

She remembered how appreciative she had felt when experienced riders mentored or acknowledged her. She was particularly grateful to Joe Fargis and Conrad Homfield. Joe had won Olympic team and individual gold medals in 1984, a silver team medal in the following 1988 Olympics, as well as a gold medal in the 1975 Pan Am Games and a fourth in the World Cup of 1989. Conrad Homfield had won Olympic team gold and individual silver in 1984 and the World Cup in 1985. They and others had offered her encouragement and kind words when she was just starting out. Margie welcomed the opportunity to give back and went out of her way to be helpful to junior riders. She never hesitated to offer a helping hand.

This ability to reach out to others was never more apparent than a winter day in 1992 when Margie received a call from the Virginia Make-A-Wish Foundation. "Margie, we have a fifteen-year-old girl with possibly terminal cancer. Autumn Hendershot will soon undergo chemotherapy and radiation treatment, but she probably will lose her leg. Her wish is to meet you and Daydream. Can this be arranged?"

This simple request truly inspired Margie. Her beloved second mother and mentor Mrs. Kramer had died years earlier from bone cancer—the same disease that was now threatening Autumn. "Mom, Dad, I feel as if my life has come full circle. Mrs. Kramer helped me so much. Now I can return some . . ." She paused to regain control. "You know what I mean. I can't believe how brave Autumn is! Even facing the amputation of her leg, she's determined to continue riding. She's just amazing!"

Margie planned the day carefully. Autumn had pictures taken with Daydream, and then Margie asked if she'd like to ride him. Autumn's eyes opened wide. "I've got posters of him. I've seen him on TV. I can't believe this!"

But that wasn't the only planned event. "Autumn, I'd like you to meet some special people who think you're pretty terrific," Margie told her. "These two good-looking men are world-class riders, Michael Matz and Greg Best, and this pretty little gal is Julie Krone. She's the only woman jockey to ever win one of the Triple Crown races—the Belmont Stakes." Autumn looked from one rider to another and managed to give each one a little nod and a wider smile with each acknowledgment.

Shown here in 1992, Autumn Hendershot and Margie with Daydream and Sebastian represented a story in courage as Virginia's Make-A-Wish Foundation granted Autumn's wish.

Later in the year, Margie and several of the other riders surprised the young equestrienne with the purchase of a horse Autumn had long admired. As they watched this courageous young girl master both her physical challenges and the readjustment of her riding technique to accommodate the prosthesis, they, too, felt elated by her success. As for us, when we read Autumn's mother's letter to our daughter, we had difficulty seeing the words through our tears. "Margie," Mrs. Beck wrote, "your kindness and positive attitude have done so much toward helping my daughter go into remission."

Like true champions, each rider—Margie and Autumn—continued for many years to admire and encourage the other. However, life and circumstances change, and almost a decade would pass before they would meet again.

Margie was so impressed with the Make-A-Wish Foundation that she arranged for all the profits of her poster sales to be donated to this organization. The demand for these horse-and-rider pictures surprised us. Irv and I watched adults and children stand in line while Margie for as long as two and often three hours signed posters and spent time talking and laughing with her fans. Co-workers and friends asked us as well to intercede for them when they wanted these mementos.

"My niece is having a *quince*. Any chance of getting an autographed copy of Margie's poster?"

"My son's best friend thinks Margie is one gutsy lady. He saw her ride with three broken ribs. Can her inscription read 'To David' and we'll surprise him at his graduation?"

"My grandparents follow Margie on ESPN, and watched her become the first rider ever to place first, second, third, fourth, and fifth in a single Grand Prix class. I'd like a poster for Christmas."

Appearances on local and national television brought their own share of surprises. After an interview with Joan Lunden on *Good Morning America*, Margie was delighted to hear her special request. "My daughter is a huge fan of yours. She was so impressed when you won *thirteen* Grand Prix in a single season. She'd be thrilled if we made a tape right now with your wishing her a happy bat mitzvah."

The March 1992 *Horse Show* magazine spotlighted Margie on Saluut II as AHSA/Hertz Equestrian of the Year. Photographer: *James Parker*

Margie also enjoyed the easy bantering among the riders. When she won an unprecedented first through fifth in the Rolex AGA Music City Grand Prix, the rider who had come in sixth teased her. "When my owner asks me how I did, I'll just tell him I came in right after Margie."

After a big 1994 show in Palm Beach, we expected Margie's report. When a phone call came from Steve instead I could barely breathe. The strain in his voice placed us immediately on guard. "Are you both there?" He struggled for the words.

"Please . . . don't worry. Margie is conscious now, but . . . but . . . we almost lost her in the ambulance . . . her heart stopped beating." My legs buckled under me, and I sank into a nearby chair. I heard Irv struggling for control, asking for the details. Shock later kept us from remembering too much about the conversation, but we learned that a horse had fallen with her, stepped on her chest and back, yet miraculously she was still alive.

We hurried up to Palm Beach and entered her hospital room. A humongous stuffed bear dominated the bed. The heavy scent of roses, gloxinias, and many mixed floral arrangements mingled with the smell of disinfectant. Gaily-colored balloons rose like silent sentinels in the midst of the animated group of visiting friends. When we finally had her all to ourselves, we asked, "Okay, Margie, how do you *really* feel?"

"Well, it only hurts when I breathe."

"What does the doctor say?"

"Several ribs are broken and several more are cracked. The stitches start in the middle of my back and continue to the middle of my front. He said I must not ride for six months."

At the end of a month and a half, Margie returned to competition.

"Please tell us you're entering fewer Grand Prix events," we begged.

"Mom, Dad, I'm doing what I feel I must." We had learned long ago when to retreat. Gradually, the look of pain left her eyes and the weekly reports filled once again with tales of successful shows and future plans.

"Dad, how much money do I have available? Can you and Mom come up to West Palm Beach on Sunday? I want you to see some property I'm looking at. Steve has already seen it and thinks it's great."

"You sound excited. What's going on?"

"Hopefully, there's going to be a *real* Gladewinds Farm, not just one on paper."

We were in the midst of the holiday whirl of 1994 when Margie and Steve came for a special visit. Our beaming daughter waltzed in, held up her left hand, and showed us the beautiful diamond-and-gold symbol of their

The November 1994 *Horse Play* magazine and writer Lisa Kiser caught Margie (shown on Saluut II) between paperwork, arrangements, flights, pupils, and Grand Prix going "at the speed of light" and marveled at her pace. The article included her mounting number of wins and "A Month in the Life of Margie Goldstein." Photographer: *Crowell Haden Jr.*

91

December 24, 1994—"Will you marry me?"

engagement. "We knew you'd want to know as soon as possible."

A grinning Steve added, "I know you think it's been a long time coming, but some things are worth waiting for."

We looked at the radiant pair before us and nodded our agreement; then Irv and I hugged, kissed, and congratulated them. When the initial excitement subsided, I added, "Margie is a lot more patient than I'd have been, but we can't imagine a better choice. Steve, you're everything we would want for Margie, and we welcome you as another son."

That year, Hanukkah for us, Christmas for Steve's parents, we had a particularly happy celebration. Throughout the sixteen years that Margie and Steve had known each other, the two sets of parents had much to say about the status of their children's relationship. We called Mary and Rudy Engle, who were then living in Texas, and the four of us joked about the "longest courtship on record."

Mary remarked, "I was getting ready to light a fire under that son of ours. What took them so long!"

I didn't argue. "I'd have been long gone, but Margie has more patience than I. She thinks no one on this planet measures up to your son."

Plans for the wedding began. "How many additions does that make?" The list grew with every passing day. "Margie, we don't even recognize some of these names. Who are they?"

"I know. Steve and I are beginning to feel overwhelmed. My clients and some of the people who attend the circuit are telling us they plan to show up at our wedding—invited or not."

When the list seemed destined to reach five hundred guests, the apprehensive couple approached us. "What if we just eloped?"

Our reply came quickly: "You know how long we've waited for this!"

"That's what we thought, too. No, we were talking about an elopement with just our closest friends and family. Look at this brochure of Grand Cayman Island. Doesn't it look like a perfect place for a wedding? And you know everybody. We'll all have a great time."

At first the idea seemed slightly bizarre, but so did the thought of a sit-down dinner for five hundred. "Okay, Margie and Steve, you've convinced us. We'll have an island wedding and a separate wedding reception here in Miami where we've already paid a deposit."

We renewed our efforts to find a qualified official, photographers, music, and a suitable site for the ceremony and the celebration. Our anxious bride-to-be asked, "Do you have a place reserved?"

I answered, "Well, we went to the Caymans' Chamber of Commerce here in Miami. They gave us several names, but we can't always reach them by phone."

The next time we saw Margie, she was lugging a large package. "What's this?" Irv inquired.

"I thought maybe you could fax the places easier than trying to call them" came the helpful reply. We sent out inquiries. We received pictures, prices, menus, maps, and brochures by return mail. And just to be sure, I called the department of records at the federal courthouse to make certain the ceremony was legal in the United States.

Now came the time for the wedding dress. Sherri, who would be the matron of honor, knew how much her best friend hated shopping, so she made an appointment for both of them to buy their dresses. While she cut my hair at her Dixie Highway beauty salon, Shear Limit, she recounted the experience. "Your daughter is impossible! She tried on one dress and said,

'That's it.' I practically forced her to try on two more. The third one looked so spectacular, everyone in the store came to admire her. I had to run back to my shop, so I left her to buy shoes on her own. They're such a terrific couple. I can't wait to see them married already! You and Irv must be counting the days."

"We are! We are!" I replied.

But I almost missed the entire wedding.

For one week prior to our plane's departure, I lay in bed, alternately soaked in perspiration or shaking with chills. "Irv, how am I going to pack for tomorrow? I can barely move!"

"I've called your doctor. Let's see what he can do to help."

And help he did. He told me I was over the worst of the flu and gave me medication to keep my nose unclogged for the flight the following day. By the time we reached the hotel in the Grand Caymans, I could feel my strength returning.

With the arrival of each guest, the level of excitement rose. Depending on interest and temperament, adults and children selected activities of their choice. The athletes in the group, spurred by Steve's love of water sports, chose snorkeling, parasailing, and scuba diving. The sightseers explored the island on land or on sea. And for those of us who simply wanted to rest or recuperate, the beaches and lagoons beckoned. When we all came together, everyone had a story to tell.

We met often. Margie and Steve invited the group to the Comedy Club on Friday evening. The comedians had a field day with the couple who had dated for seventeen years, but Margie replied with a reasonably straight face, "We don't believe in rushing into anything."

The wedding was set for 5 P.M. on the next day, Sunday, November 18, 1995. One hour prior to the wedding, our suite buzzed with activity. Sherri came over to help Margie with her hair. Margie was rearranging our carefully worked-out seating plan. The taxi was late and we were running out of time. Irv called the taxi company only to find out other guests had taken the first cab. He ordered a second car and, wanting no more hijacks, arranged to meet them in a hidden alley behind the hotel.

I turned around to check on Margie. My eyes misted. "You look . . . you look . . . absolutely gorgeous." Her brown eyes sparkled. Her normally light brown hair was flecked with sun-bleached gold. Her formfitting, white satin and pearl-encrusted lace, ankle-length dress hugged her curves smoothly, then flared out in a graceful swirl. She wore a shoulder-length veil, my borrowed earrings, and the traditional—but hidden—blue garter.

Suddenly, I began to laugh. "Margie, what are you doing?"

Realizing that she could not walk in her unaccustomed high-heeled shoes, she was busy stuffing tissues into the toes of the oversized footwear. "I guess I should have tried them on before buying them. I just hate taking the time to shop."

Sherri looked over and shrugged. "I told you she was impossible!"

I answered, "I guess Margie forgot she wanted to wear boots to her wedding."

The taxi finally arrived, and we rushed to our designated area in the restaurant. "Irv, what happened to this old building? It's lovely—positively aglow with the sun's reflection."

We looked outside from a hidden porch in the restaurant. Margie was smiling. "I can't believe how beautiful everything is! Thank you both."

A delicate white gazebo had been set up on one side of the pier under the wild pines. Steve, his best man, Jim Kenney, and the clergyman were waiting there. Behind them, the guests already were seated, with an aisle left open for our upcoming walk. We could hear the music faintly over the sound of the ocean lapping at the large rocks below the pier. The sky's horizon blazed red, pink, and orange hues as the setting sun's reflection danced upon the blue-and-gold water.

"I don't think any one of us will forget this beautiful place, but look at your groom, Margie. He looks a little worried." Steve's strong, handsome face was strained with concern for our late arrival. He pushed up the sleeves of his island-formal white shirt to look at his watch.

Mark and Eddie had seen us arrive and were waiting to lead me to my seat. I placed a hand into each of my son's arms and looked at their familiar, well-loved faces. "How lucky I am to be escorted by the two best-looking men on the island!" I told them.

We took our seats and turned to watch the rest of the wedding party. First came the brown-eyed, brown-haired flower girl, carefully dropping rose petals along the path. Pretty Suzi, our nine-year-old granddaughter,

November 18, 1995—"I will! I will!"

looked like a younger version of her aunt Margie as she walked slowly down the aisle and then joined her parents. A look of relief passed over her face as she sat down. Next came Sherri, radiant in her flowered, festive dress. Just before the bride and her father stepped into the aisle, we heard the swelling notes of the wedding march. Margie smiled broadly, but the mixture of many complex feelings flitted across Irv's face.

The ceremony pleased the families of both religions. The clergyman, a Universalist, spoke of the love and the similar virtues that bound Steve and Margie. His elegant accent served as a reminder that the Caymans were a part of Great Britain, as did the marriage certificate we read later. Dr. and Mrs. Steven Engle were now husband and wife by order of Her Majesty Queen Elizabeth II.

When the reverend announced, "You may kiss the bride," a well-timed breeze lifted Margie's veil from her face and over her head. Every time we later viewed the video, she would say, "Watch! Isn't that amazing? I can't believe the wind did that!"

Chef Tell enhanced his reputation with the dinner that followed the ceremony. Steve was delighted. "I've been in many places and many countries, but this is the single best meal I've ever had." Margie, too excited to eat her entire meal, had it wrapped for the following day. The guests toasted and teased the happy couple well into the night.

When the honeymooners returned, Margie moved her residence to Steve's. But the two of them continued to travel back and forth between Wellington and North Miami, their work-related barns, the out-of-town sites that comprised the show-jumping circuit, plus the racetracks where Steve began work at daybreak. We could not help worrying. "It sure would be great if the two of you could slow down. You look so tired."

Steve was also attending classes to acquire additional training in acupuncture and chiropractic medicine for large animals. Margie proudly told us how well these skills served him. "Steve went to one of his owner's barn. A horse named TP was in terrible pain. He reared whenever Steve tried to touch him. Steve got two others to hold him while he began the chiropractic manipulation. In the middle of his struggles, TP suddenly realized he was *not* hurting and placed his head on Steve's shoulder. You could almost hear him saying 'Hey! That feels great.' The next time Steve went to the barn, TP ran in from the pasture and put his head on Steve's shoulder. Who says horses can't talk?"

Not only did Margie benefit from these services, but other riders did as well. Steve found himself flying to more and more "horse house calls" when his wife was on the circuit or driving to the many barns where Margie had rented stalls for her owners' horses.

In an effort to relieve some of the complications in their lives, Margie turned to family and friends for time she just didn't have. "Dad, would you work out the finances to see how much we can invest in Gladewinds?" "Alan, thanks for lending me your secretary and for expediting the legalities!" "Lea, thanks for taking care of my clothes shopping."

After a few years of frustrations, setbacks, and some financial assistance from the family, the barn became a reality. When we first walked through the brand-new, beautiful building with its thirty stalls and attached apartment for the horses' grooms, we gazed in wonder. Burnt orange clay tiles spread protectively over the roof. Green shutters opened wide to let the horses enjoy the cool breezes. Gazing through two of the windows were our old veterans from the early days, Saluut II and Daydream, now living a life of leisurely retirement. The floors and white walls were spotless. Newly painted white fencing surrounded ten acres of leveled land. A brightly colored sign proclaimed to one and all, GLADEWINDS FARM: MARGIE GOLDSTEIN ENGLE, OWNER.

Sherri and her little four-year-old daughter, Brittany, had taken the tour with us. Her eyes filled with delight for her friend and she inquired, "Did you ever think you'd see this day?"

I shook my head, unable to answer. My thoughts had drifted back to Dorothy Kramer and how proud she would be. "Gladewinds will live forever, Margie, because I'm *giving* the name to you. I know you'll never bring anything but honor to it."

CHAPTER TWELVE

Grand Prix Days

As THE WEEKLY WINS ACCUMULATED, the yearly standings rose as well.

Annually and with great pleasure, Goldstein friends and families listened to the Palm Beach or Tampa show-jumping announcer intone: "Can you believe it? Only Gold Medal World Champion [1986] Katie Monahan Prudent has been Rider of the Year three times. With this AGA 1994 win, Margie Goldstein joins the masters!"

"Ladies and gentlemen, Margie Goldstein Engle has broken another record. Our clear winner for the 1995 AGA Rider of the Year is now taking her victory gallop around the course."

"The last rider, the first clear round! Ladies and gentlemen, there will be no jump-off. Margie Goldstein Engle, the first four-time winner, is now the first *five*-time AGA Rider of the Year!"

This five-time feat has been unmatched in the history of the sport: 1989, 1991, 1994, 1995, 1996—the American Grand Prix Association can be very proud of this true champion. In 1999, 2000–2001, and 2003, Margie would break still more records and earn a total of *eight* AGA Rider of the Year Awards!

We sat around our dining room table in May 1997. "Well, little sister, who would have thought it?" Eddie said. "National Grand Prix League Rider of the Year Award for three years, the Hertz Equestrian of the Year Award, now this! Do you have any more surprises up your sleeve?"

"Just this one. Happy birthday, Eddie! I won the Rolex Grand Prix in Germantown, and I've been saving this watch for you. I hope you like it."

The guests at the Goldstein dinner table laughed. "You should see your face, Ed. You seem a little startled."

"I've been admiring yours and Steve's watches, Margie, but I never expected to have a Rolex of my own."

"What kind of wife and sister would I be if I couldn't keep you both in good times?"

"Margie," groaned her nephew Matt. "Good *times*? You can do better than that."

The wins are so easy to accept; the losses must be borne with grace. Margie started 1996 with a herniated disk in a spine so filled with pain that, for several weeks, she was barely able to move, much less compete. Although two doctors urged surgery, Dr. Mark Brown at Jackson Memorial Hospital was that rare surgeon who didn't turn to a scalpel as the first solution. "Margie, the bed rest you were forced to take was something your body desperately needed. Now I want you to try these exercise techniques." He handed her a list. "You really should give up horse riding, because the constant pounding on your vertebrae is not helping the curvature in your spine."

Margie started to interrupt, but Dr. Brown continued. "I've already heard that you'll compete no matter what I say, so we'll order a back brace that you must wear when you ride and when you feel the first signs of pain." Margie followed his directions carefully and returned to successful competition.

We met two of Margie's owners who took great pride in the quality of their stable. Ben Al Saud, a member of the royal family of Saudi Arabia, was short, darkly good-looking, with a vividly hued parrot on his shoulder appropriately named Colors. By his side stood a tall, beautiful blonde. Behind him was his truck—the most colorful I had ever seen. Cotton-candy clouds were painted on a sky-blue background. Mounted hurdle-jumping horses that Margie rode for him had been airbrushed to match Ben's image. In large multihued letters was painted RAINBOW FARMS. He graciously took us to see his favorite horses: Land of Kings, a

Sebastian, owned by Katherine Chope and then Frances Snodgrass, a 16.2-hand gray stallion, was very careful and quick across the ground. He would sometimes jump past his arc, so they practiced often with canter rails and short combinations. He won many Grand Prix Speed Classes. Photographer: *Vern O'Neill* ©

Lacasta, owned by Robert Pergament, wore a bonnet or ear-muffs because he was easily startled by loud noises and they helped muffle the sound. He was a bit difficult, but very scopey and brave. He had his own jumping style, and although it wasn't perfect form, it worked for him and he attained success over seven years in Grand Prix competition.

101

Caribbean Queen, owned by Rainbow Farms (Prince Ben Al Saud). At 17.1 hands, this Westphalian mare had a huge stride and lots of scope. Margie began riding her at four years old, and her biggest problem was dealing with her long stride and size in combinations and tight lines. Many hours of flat-work contributed to her development in collecting and shortening her stride. Also, they constantly worked on tight combinations and adjustability approaching the fences. For a large, big-boned horse, Caribbean Queen was sensitive, but very obliging with loads of talent.
Photographer: *Cheryl Bender ©*

1996   Land of Kings, a very large Holsteiner stallion owned by Rainbow Farms (Prince Ben Al Saud), was scopey but had a bit of an attitude. He could get cold to ride, so Margie worked on keeping him fit and rode him aggressively to keep him from trying to get away with anything he could. Among his outstanding wins were Lake Placid, Upperville, and Newport Grand Prix.
Photographer: *Cheryl Bender ©*

Power and Speed Magazine in 1994 recognized Margie (shown on Hidden Creek's Aristo) as Rolex/NGL Rider of the Year, 1992 and 1993. The accompanying article also described Margie receiving the award from surprise presenter, Autumn Hendershot. Aristo, owned by Dr. Katherine Chope and Hidden Creek Farms (Mike Polaski), became spooky at everything around the jumps and everywhere else. He wore the fuzzies on the side of the bridle and on his nosebands to help channel his concentration onto the task at hand. As spooked as he was, he was still brave at the jumps and did well in all types of classes, from Speed to Puissance to Grand Prix. Photographer: *Gary Benson* ©

17-hand white stallion, and Caribbean Queen, a 17.1-hand Westphalian blood bay mare.

"Margie, considering the situation in the Mideast, how do you and Ben get along?"

She ignored my implications. "Other riders have asked me that. We started out with distinct and differing opinions about many things, including the treatment of the horses. But we've learned to accommodate each other. Now that he has confidence in me, I do the training, decide how many times the horses will enter—I don't want the horses too tired—and what classes each is capable of. He continues to warm up the horses just before we show them, but only on the flat and only a couple of jumps."

She continued, "Ben likes gaudy saddle pads, leg wrappings in rainbow colors, and multicolored reins. Some of the more conservative riders laugh when we go in the ring. They tell me that there's no way they'd ride his 'carousel horses.' But many fans want to take pictures of me atop one of Ben's steeds. They *love* the flashy effect!"

Still, there were times when Mideast met West and sparks flew. A tired Ben drove in from one horse show to check out his stalls for the next event in Wellington. There he encountered an equally exhausted groom of Margie's.

"Whose trunks are these in front of my stalls?" he demanded.

"I'll get to them as soon as I can. At the moment, I've got other work that must be done."

Ben fumed. "You'll do them *now*!" He used a few choice Arabic epithets. "Where's Margie? I'm calling her this minute."

"You are *not*! She's in Arizona," the groom replied. Then she locked the door to the tack room that housed the only phone in the barn.

Ben shoved her to the ground, smashed the tack room door, and called Margie. "I want this girl fired!" He launched into a litany of complaints. "And don't you dare back up that groom over me!"

Margie held the receiver away from her ear as one, then the other, shouted out his and her side of the story. She listened until their anger subsided and then made suggestions to each combatant.

"You just can't get in his face when you're talking to him. Don't worry. You're not being fired, but let Ben know that everything will be taken care of before the show begins," Margie said to the groom.

Then she spoke to her furious client. "Ben, you can't treat people like that. All the trunks will be moved, but no more shoving and no more shouting. We have a show to win and we need help *now* with Caribbean Queen and Land of Kings."

The reminder of the competition and his prized horses calmed Ben, for he settled down and within a few days paid to have the door replaced.

When she told us this story later, Margie jokingly said that the only recognized royalty around the barn were the horses. Prince and provider worked out their minor disagreements and, in the process, learned mutual respect.

In 1998, a transatlantic flight from New York to London exploded in the air and crashed near the shore of Long Island. The sad wreckage of human remains provided few answers for a shocked nation.

Margie asked us, "Did you hear about the airplane that crashed after taking off from New York? We think Ben was aboard. His family will not confirm or deny it."

"Oh, no! We're so sorry."

"Yeah, I am, too. All I can think of is how hard he struggled to fit into such a different world from what he knew, the dinners and good times we shared after a Grand Prix. Oh, how he loved his horses!"

The great loss of life and inability to accept or find answers made the crash a tragedy. Margie had lost a close and valued friend, and that made it real.

We met Mike Polaski, a tall, muscular horse owner imposing in his all-black outfit, at one of the shows in Tampa. "Tell us about Mike, honey. He seems to be quiet, but taking in everything."

"Mike runs a successful insurance business—Specialty Underwriters, Inc.—in Wisconsin. He's always been interested in horses and has a beautiful—impeccable taste—stable there where he's hoping to breed jumpers, not hunters, at the top level. I met him a few years ago at a horse show in Wisconsin. He's had several trainers before me, but the horses they bought for him weren't competitive enough for Mike."

"How so?"

"He runs the stable, Hidden Creek, as a business—buying and selling—but he wants a strong string of horses that can compete at the Grand Prix level. He's willing to do what it takes to have a quality string while he's waiting for his own horses to breed Grand Prix offspring. And he really takes an active interest in the competition no matter where we travel. Also, he likes to decide which horse will be competing."

As we watched Margie ride Hidden Creek's Alvaretto and Hidden Creek's Laurel, two of Mike's recent purchases, we marveled at their strength and grace, which indicated excellent potential.

In June 1996 with Olympic competition almost complete and Caribbean Queen in second spot for one of the top four positions, a despondent Margie called. "Mom, Dad, would you believe lightning just struck for the second time?"

"Margie, are you all right? We can barely hear you."

Her voice sounded flat and low. "Remember when Saluut's leg was injured just before the last Olympic Trials?"

"That's not something we're likely to forget! Oh, Lord! What happened?"

"In the horse van on the way to the show, Caribbean Queen injured her leg. For me there will be no Olympics. I . . . I just can't believe it."

What irony! Here was Margie, ranked number one in the United States, but unable to represent her country in the most exciting and best-known event in the world. "Oh, honey. I wish we could help. You've dreamed of this for so long."

"I know. The Europeans think we're crazy. Their national equestrian committees simply identify their four outstanding riders and one alternate. They say we wear out our horses by having an intense period of elimination during the trials. But . . ." Her voice trailed off.

Yet if there are disappointments in sports, there are times to celebrate as well. Margie had competitive horses she loved and who were anxious to jump. She ended 1996 by riding Mike's Holsteiner chestnut gelding, Hidden Creek's Alvaretto, to the number one position: AGA Horse of the Year. She described Al as a little horse (15.3 1/2 hands) who thought he was big. "He's quick and careful, compact and feisty—a spunky, gutsy little horse who loves to jump."

And just to enhance the pleasure, she rode Hidden
behind him to the number two spot: 1996 AGA Reser
Year. In the AHSA standings, she rode Laurel to the r
with Alvaretto closing in as Reserve Champion. Margi
". . . the most consistent horse I've ever known. She holds the record for
the most first-round clean rounds, for the AGA and all events, with seventeen in a row, and that included many of the nation's toughest shows."

When he accompanied his horses to the winner's circle at the AGA
1996 final event in Palm Beach, Mike—hardly the quiet man we had first
thought him to be—bubbled over with pride!

In 1997, Margie qualified to represent the United States in Nation's
Cup competitions in Italy, Switzerland, the Netherlands, France, and
Germany. Both Steve and Mike were there to cheer her on, and she
didn't disappoint them. The Grand Prix and Leading Rider international
events added up to her computer ranking as the Leading Lady Rider in the
world. The 1998 World Cup in Helsinki clinched it when Margie won several events during the week and narrowly missed the number one position
at the final Grand Prix. In fact, Margie held the title of the World's Leading Lady Rider for a proud record of 115 weeks.

Hearing about the Helsinki win, her brother Eddie said, "That's the
first time I remember Margie being satisfied with second place."

One of Margie's fans taped the Grand Prix in Rome. Although all the
announcing was in Italian, every now and then we heard our daughter's
name. The camera panned the stands as an estimated thirty-five thousand
people enthusiastically supported their favorite riders. They loudly cheered
during the jump-off when a few competitors with clear rounds narrowed
down to only one show jumper. We had no trouble recognizing three
words from the announcer: *Margie Goldstein Engle.*

"The Star-Spangled Banner" never sounded so stirring or so beautiful
to our ears as at that moment when the camera focused upon our daughter's smiling face and the flag of our United States superimposed behind
her image. I commented to Irv, "Gee, I wish I could understand what
they're saying."

I agreed with his reply. " Sometimes words are not necessary."

* * *

Acclaim, accident, triumph, tragedy. Would we ever get used to the pattern?

"Margie, are you all right now? How did it happen?" The call came in early July 1998.

"I can't believe I was so stupid. It had rained so badly that I withdrew my horses from the competition. I didn't want them to be hurt. But one of the horses we sold to a junior rider was giving his new owner problems and I was trying to iron out the kinks. When the horse skidded suddenly because of the wet ground, I was thrown into the metal cups on the jump."

"The *metal* cups? Please, I can't bear it—what happened?"

"My nose was splayed open. Fortunately, the doctor on call in Lake Placid was able to put me back together. He used thirty-six stitches to sew up my nose and lip. Steve watched him and said he was very good."

"How horrible! You weren't able to compete in the World Championship Trials the following day."

"Well . . ."

"Oh, Margie, how could you?"

"I was able to have a clear first round, but I just did okay in the jump-off."

Margie was showing both Hidden Creek's Alvaretto and Hidden Creek's Glory for the trials. She lay down on a cot in the tack room between jumps. Kim Tudor, president of SportsMark, Ltd., applied cold compresses. Years later, she told us, "I have always felt that Margie's life story should be made into a movie: an inspirational movie for all young kids who want to ride at any cost. Young kids who spend every waking moment trying to convince their parents to turn their suburban garage into a two-stall barn. I began to believe it would be a truly *great* movie after watching Margie ride during the trials in Lake Placid."

Kim told us about a conversation with a group of people recalling thrilling moments in sports and their admiration for the little gymnast competing through the pain of a twisted ankle. "Not to take anything away from Kerri Strug's accomplishment, but—a twisted ankle? I told them about Margie, beaten, sore, and unable to see or stand up, lifted into the saddle so that she could come out on top during the World Championship Trials. Having to lie down between rounds because she didn't have

In 1994, Hidden Creek's Laurel (16.2 hands), a very sensitive mare with a classic jumping style, reigned as the princess of the barn. She was more delicate than most of the horses both physically and mentally. She required slow, relaxing work, but was definitely worth it. As sweet and easy as she was around the barn, she became nervous in the schooling and crowded areas. Margie tried not to exert too much pressure either in her jumping or with flatwork when she was with other horses. Once in the ring and by herself, she was adjustable and went around a jumper course like a hunter. Laurel went on to win the Hampton Classic two years in a row, AGA Championships, 1996 AHSA Horse of the Year, 1996 AGA Reserve Champion, 1997 Grand Prix in Rome, Nation's Cup in Montreal, and second place in the World Cup Finals in Helsinki, Finland.
Photographer: *Vern O'Neill* ©

Among his many accomplishments, Hidden Creek's Alvaretto won AGA Horse of the Year 1996, the 1997 Grand Prix in Arnheim, Holland, and the American Invitational 1999. Al presented a sweet nature around the barn and loved the days he showed. At 15.3 hands, "Big Al" belied his small stature with a lot of scope, heart, and much energy. Sometimes the energy caused him to get too excited and too quick to the jumps, so Margie added strides to slow him and keep him from getting flat. If a line walked a long five strides for another horse, she did six strides with Alvaretto.
Photographer: *Vern O'Neill* ©

109

Nov. 1997   *Practical Horseman* magazine recognized the U.S. Equestrian Team for outstanding wins in international competition. Margie also had individual wins in Grand Prix in Aachen, Rome, St. Gallen, and Arnheim. A year earlier, writer Sandra Olinyak of *Practical Horseman* magazine identified the many reasons for Margie's success, including her kindness and concern for the horses she rode and the people she came in contact with: her clients, fellow riders, friends, and fans. Her students say she makes them believe in themselves. The cover shot shows Margie on Hidden Creek's Alveretto. Photographer: *Arnd Bronkhorst*

2000   *State Line Tack Catalog*, sponsors of USET, features Margie and Laurel on its millennium cover.   Photographer: *Bob Langrish*

the strength to stand. Unable to take painkillers. Thrown back up into the saddle for another clear round. Now, that is heroic! That is a story!"

When Irv and I saw both the accident and Margie's mangled face on the delayed broadcasts, we could barely contain our tears. Steve insisted that she come home for time to recover. During those weeks in the summer of '98, we found looking at Margie painful.

From August 5 to 8, Margie and her USET teammates took part in the do-or-die 1999 Pan American Games in Winnipeg, Canada. They were on a mission to earn gold or silver in order for the USET to qualify for participation in the 2000 Olympic Games. Margie on Alvaretto, Peter Wylde on Macanudo De Niro, Allison Firestone on Arne De La Barre, and Leslie Burr Howard on Clover Leaf rode close rounds with Brazil. The lead volleyed back and forth between the two teams with the Brazilians ending up with the gold. The United States, however, had reached its goal, the silver medal that earned them a ticket to Sydney, Australia.

Jewish Women magazine featured Margie as one of the top ten women in the world for the year 5760 (1999–2000). Margie was so far ahead in the computer rankings for her *sixth* AGA Rider of the Year (1999) Award that the programs in both Palm Beach and Tampa featured her on the cover and in their contents before the final event on April 8, 2000. I looked at the cover on the Tampa program and noted, "Irv, will you look at that? The cover shot of Margie features one very large, very black eye!"

"Margie, we're going to be in Australia and New Zealand besides stopping in LA to see Mark, Cindy, and the kids," I told her in early March 1999. "It will be the longest time we've ever been away, so Dad will need to prepare your payroll information in advance."

"When is this?"

"We'll be gone all the month of April."

"Then you'll miss the American Invitational."

"It's usually in March. What happened? Cousin Sue has already let us know our room is ready and waiting for us."

"This may be the last year it's in Tampa. The date was changed."

Budweiser American Invitational April 1, 2000
presented by The Tampa Tribune

Margie Engle and Hidden Creek's Alvaretti
defending
Budweiser American Invitational Champio
and
Five Time AGA Rider of the Year

photo © Cheryl Bender

AGA National Championship
presented by FedEx, Jaguar, The Tampa Tribune April 8, 2000

The April 8, 2000, *Budweiser American Invitational Program* featured Margie and Alvaretto on the cover. As loyal, longtime sponsors, Budweiser's support of show jumping as a sport has been greatly appreciated by the entire horse-jumping population. She's shown here defending her American Invitational 1999 award, but Margie and the team also brought home a team silver at the Pan Am Games in Canada and the first-place SCIO Nation's Cup in New York.
Photographer: *Cheryl Bender ©*

113

We were in the middle of an Australian rain forest in a small hotel called Silky Oaks when Margie's fax arrived. She had copied the *Tampa Tribune* article describing the event and written across the top, "At last!" Ah, the wonders of technology! In this remote little place halfway around the world, we were able to share her news.

When we arrived home in Miami, we watched the televised event, still being broadcast at several scheduled times. We knew the stress and thrill that each rider felt. The American Invitational is a prestigious and exciting Grand Prix for the thirty riders selected. Because the event is by invitation only, there is no entry fee for the competitors. The riders are limited to one horse, so they make their selection carefully.

Course designer Steve Stephens crafted his hurdles with full knowledge of the competence at this level. He arranged thirteen varied and colorful obstacles of five feet or more in height with one double combination and one triple, requiring sixteen jumps total. His triple combination was particularly difficult, because the first and third jumps included a seven-foot spread within the two-fenced oxers. The middle element in the triple included visual barriers designed to fool and confuse a horse in motion. Because Stephens was among those who believe horses are color blind, he had the top part painted white, thus fading the poles into the background, and the bottom part painted blue with a distracting water hazard underneath. Following the thirteenth obstacle, a liverpool (an extra-wide water hazard with a rail over the water) reflected the glare of the floodlights at the evening event. This can, and does, spook the horses.

The TV panned the cavernous new Raymond James Stadium. At each end of the bowl, two huge television screens provided clear coverage and instant replay or extended coverage of this much-heralded event. A mammoth pirate ship with its pioneer pier homes and warehouses dominated the entire west side of the stadium and served as a reminder of Tampa's early history. A column of mounted police, two abreast, paraded onto the field with the American flags they carried whipping in the breeze. The stage was set.

Margie had alternately tested and rested Hidden Creek's Alvaretto prior to this competition and felt he was equal to the task. As she walked the course with the other riders, she planned her strategy. Many sportswriters have described her as one of the most cerebral strategists, and she had no intention of disappointing them or herself. Her advantage would be that she had earned the right to ride close to the end. (Riders go in reverse order of their current standings.) Her disadvantage would be that she would be followed by three of the nation's most outstanding riders.

Twenty-four attempts preceded her. The number ten fence, a liverpool in the middle of a triple with the night lights reflecting and distracting the horses, was particularly difficult. One rider voluntarily withdrew when his horse twice refused it. Another thrilled the crowd with her clear round, but exceeded the time allowance of ninety-three seconds for a quarter-point penalty. The others disassembled one or more of the jumps. As expected, most of these knocked-down fences occurred within the triple combination. The excited fans cheered the valiant efforts and groaned with each falling rail.

Margie and Alvaretto entered the arena to a roaring welcome. His brushed chestnut body gleamed under the floodlights. As his head swung from side to side, his eyes bulged far from their sockets, making him appear to be fighting Margie's control. When he burst over the first fence, broadcaster Lysa Burke chuckled and announced, "Al is dancing tonight." Margie, knowing that Alvaretto sometimes got nervous, settled him down, trying to maintain an easy but steady gait. "Okay, Al, easy does it. Everything will be fine."

They turned to approach the fourth obstacle, an airy, three-paneled vertical designed to confuse the horse and make the rider quickly select the middle of one of the series of three poles. They cleared this penalty-producing fence. "Good boy, you're doing great!"

Margie took a fast peek at the time as they rode to the eighth obstacle. This brightly hued butterfly standard measured over six and a half feet and provided distraction for some horses. They cleared this and counted the paces to the SeaWorld obstacle with its heavy planks balanced precariously on flat cups. The slightest tap caused the plank to drop, and several competitors had heard the thud as they jumped over it. Margie steered her talented stallion upward. "I knew you could do it! Great, great, great Alvaretto!"

On to the triple combination and not one sound could be heard from the spectators. When she cleared the last element, the buzzing began. As

Margie and Alvaretto sailed over fences twelve and thirteen, the roar of the standing crowd erupted with a life of its own.

After her fault-free round, we listened to the interviewer ask her, "Only once in the history of the American Invitational has a rider won without a jump-off. What do you think your chances are to do the same?"

Her reply was realistic. "We have three riders at the top of their form coming up. Any one of them could easily overtake me."

Allison Firestone and Gustil P, an excellent duo, dropped a fence early in the round, but recovered to become the fastest of the riders with four faults. Nona Garson, equally talented, and her often-winning partner, Rhythmical, had trouble from the beginning, but continued their efforts. As they approached the middle element in the triple combination, the reflected light spooked Rhythmical and he refused the jump. Nona was thrown from her horse, expertly landed on her feet, and withdrew from the competition.

McLain Ward, 1998 Rider of the Year and the previous year's winner, entered the arena. Margie felt the camera upon her and tried hard to keep her expression neutral. McLain rode smoothly and well until he attempted the treacherous triple combination. When the pole hit the ground, the announcer's voice was drowned out by the crowd's cheering for Margie. We heard Lysa Burke over the noise in the stadium. "Finally! It couldn't happen to a nicer person."

We couldn't agree more!

CHAPTER THIRTEEN

The Olympic Goal

THE YEAR 1999 CONTINUED WITH ONE WIN AFTER ANOTHER, and Margie earned her sixth AGA Rider of the Year with ease. Still, she worried about the horses. Even though she tried to alternately compete, and then rest, her mounts, she could tell some were not going to be ready physically for

Prior to the 2000 Olympics, Denim and Diamonds in Wellington auctioned service for one day from Katie Monahan Prudent, Anne Kursinski, Leslie Burr Howard, and Margie (right to left). They raised funds in elephant-sized amounts for USET.
Photographer: *Cheryl Bender* ©

the Olympic Trials coming up the following year. No matter how well riders planned, injuries created their own time lines.

She discussed the situation with the owner of Hidden Creek Farms. "Mike, what would you think about buying another horse of Grand Prix caliber? Both Laurel and Al are still capable, but Laurel's taking a lot longer to recover than we thought and Al is getting older and needs more time between his many trials. Since next year will be a grueling one with the Olympics and all, we might be better off with a new one I saw."

Mike listened to Margie's critiques—the pros and cons of each horse she had considered. "Our best bet might be Perin," she told him. "He moves like an athlete, is scopey and careful, but the owner is asking a high price for an inexperienced horse. He had planned to show him but never did."

"Isn't that the horse you told me about last year?"

"Yes, but even then, the owner was asking too high a price. Perin's large. He stands tall at 17.1½ hands, and he likes to jump."

"If that's what you think, then go for it!"

Margie felt enormous gratitude for her supportive owner and friend. "I think he's got a lot of talent."

Irv and I saw Hidden Creek's Perin for the first time at the Palm Beach 2000 circuit. He was bay colored, of Westphalian lineage, and he looked enormous. After several performances, I said, "Irv, he looks awfully green to me. How many Sundays have we seen him show? He'll be going great and then—down comes a fence."

"Well, Margie has faith in him. That's what's important."

What Margie didn't tell us was how unfit Perin was when he arrived from Germany. We *read* about him in an interview in which Margie was quoted: "We just got him out of quarantine, and I am telling everyone how much I like this horse. So he gets here and he is so out of shape and his feet are so bad. I'm telling everyone how great he is and the poor horse couldn't trot once around the ring without gasping for breath! I couldn't jump him at first, and then I took him to the Gold Cup. Luckily Mike wasn't there to see this poor horse. When Mike showed up, he wasn't too impressed, because Perin's not even near what I had tried two years earlier. He had done nothing! He was too unfit to hack—let alone jump!"

Margie went to work, spending enormous amounts of time to help Perin reach his full potential. He had all the natural scope, carefulness, and ability that you would want in any horse. He just needed work to provide experience and ridability. Daily they practiced flatwork with emphasis on adjustability and responsiveness to the leg and hand aids.

Perin also needed to deal with his large scope. His tendency was to overjump obstacles. He would not only go too high, but also land so far out that he couldn't fit the correct number of strides into a tight combination. The determined pair practiced low gymnastics and low, tight lines. Gradually, Perin figured out that he didn't have to jump so high and so far across; the farther into a combination he landed, the harder it was for him. Perin began to look in the air at the next obstacle and back himself up. "That's what I really liked about him. He tries hard to figure things out," Margie explained. "I don't know if you noticed, but horses are better when they're free jumping than when they're mounted. So usually, the less interference from the rider, the better the horses jump."

There was a big show at the Miami Arena and two equally important events in Tampa. We attended them with the hope of seeing progress from this large, friendly horse. Irv commented, "Well, Perin is the best of the four-faulters."

"Remember what you told me?" I replied. "Margie has faith in him. She says he's very consistent for this level, and we have to remember his lack of experience."

The 2000 Olympic Trials began in the last week of June at the USET headquarters in Gladstone, New Jersey. We were happy that Steve would be with Margie, both for moral support and to take care of the horses. He promised to call us the minute each trial in the series was over.

After the first event on Wednesday, Steve's voice boomed across the wires. "Do you want to know who was the *only* clear rider today?"

My words came tumbling out. "Are you telling us what I think you are?"

"That's right. Perin rode beautifully on the most difficult course I've ever seen. Your daughter will be busy signing autographs for hours, so she'll talk to you later."

When we got off the phone, Irv and I both began exclaiming to each other. "I—I—I think this is wonderful."

"Easy does it, Mona. There's a long way to go."

On Friday, Steve called in the morning, then later that afternoon. "She's still number one! Margie is the only rider with three fault-free rounds."

On Saturday, Steve called again. "Steve, why are you calling? Is everything all right?"

He laughed. "We're in Detroit, and Margie just won the Grand Prix tonight on Reggae. Boy, is she on a roll! Just as soon as the rain stops, we're headed back to New Jersey."

Later that evening, I said to Irv, "I know I must be the world's biggest worrywart, but I sure wish they were back in Gladstone *safely*."

Sunday morning crawled slowly as we imagined what was going on in Gladstone. Finally, the phone rang. "Mark?"

"I wondered if you knew what was happening. I've searched through the Internet and I can't find how Margie did."

"What do you mean? Steve will call with the results."

"The Internet lists everyone who competed in the Trial Four show-jumping event and their scores. I've read every name. I can't find Margie's."

My thoughts leaped ahead. "Oh no, she didn't get back in time for the trials."

Mark's shock now matched our own. Irv said, "We can't stay on the phone. Steve is probably trying to call."

The next couple of hours were sheer torture. First, her dad and I worried that Margie and Steve had been delayed by the weather and had never made it back to the trials. "She'll be out—no Olympics. Not again. I can't believe this."

I tried to distract myself with a book, but I kept reading the same paragraph over and over and was unable to stay focused. Irv tried to pick up news on the Internet, but was unsuccessful. He remembered that the phone line was tied in to the computer and we didn't want to miss Steve's call, so he gave up on this source. When he came into the family room to turn on the news, I feared the worse. "Do you think there was an accident?" I said silent prayers for their safety.

Long minutes turned into longer hours. "I can't stand it. I'm going to try to reach Steve."

Irv cautioned. "Bad news travels quickly. If anything happened, they'd let us know. Don't tie up the phone."

At this point, my nerves were raw. "I *must* do something. I'll call on Steve's phone."

When his telephone answering machine began the recording, I was too choked up to leave a message. Next I called on Margie's cell phone. The laughter in our son-in-law's voice as he began with "I was just going to call you" was reassuring.

"Steve, we hadn't heard from you and—of course—thought the worse. Is Margie all right? What's going on?"

"Everything is fine *now*. Perin was really scared when he twisted his shoe in the middle of Trial Four this morning, but—amazingly—he kept on going. We've been quite busy—getting everything rebuilt and putting padding between his hoof and the shoe. They allow you to drop your lowest score during these five events, so that worked out. He was still shaken up for the trial that followed this afternoon, but Margie managed to bring him under control with only nine and a quarter faults. She has to stay in the top four. She's now number three in the Olympic standings."

"But they're okay?"

Margie called us back later to reassure us that all was well. "Perin is so brave. I thought he had thrown his shoe, but I felt terrible when I saw it was still attached and had twisted into his hoof. But why were *you* so worried?"

I repeated the series of circumstances, and then added, "Why did you feel you had to go to Detroit in the middle of the Olympic Trials?"

"Mom, besides Mike's horses, I rode Reggae for Robert Pergament."

"Yes?"

"You know how supportive and wonderful he's been all through the years."

"But—"

"I bet you've forgotten what happened in Southampton."

"You're right. What happened there?"

"Mr. Pergament was in the hospital recovering from an operation. I was showing his horse, Global. He got special permission from his doctor to come to the show grounds just so he could see us ride—good thing we

2000 Reggae, owned by Robert Pergament, became one of the fastest horses around. He loved to show and was a real winner. He didn't need much jumping between shows—he knew his job and just needed to stay fit. He's still showing and winning with Cayce Harrison in the amateur jumper division. Photographer: *James Parker*

won. He was so happy—he went back to the hospital and told everyone that's what he needed to recover."

"But you could have missed the trials—how could you take a chance like that?"

"I was showing some of Mike's horses also—Jones won a third. Mike sent his private plane when he heard that we couldn't make the commercial plane back. You didn't have to worry."

I felt arguing further was useless. "Margie, I guess that's our job as parents. What surprised us was how upset your brother was. When Mark and Cindy come to the second half of the trials in August, you're going to have a pair of very nervous fans in the stands." Oh, did those words prove to be prophetic!

During the next several weeks, we kept the phone lines very busy. "Where are you this week, Margie?" "You're joining Margie *where*, Steve? How are you keeping up with the track and your practice?"

Steve responded, "I can't keep up. I finally had to give up the horses at the track, because of all the travels with Margie. When I'm back in Wellington, I only have time to go to the barns."

"Steve, I hope you feel as good about that as we do. Her dad and I feel a lot more at ease when we know Margie is with you. She told us the other riders appreciate your taking care of their horses, too. You can't be in three places at once. Two's enough."

In the beginning of August, the second half of the trials began at Del Mar, California. From seventy-six competitors, there were now twelve. A few days before the competition began, Allison Firestone's horse developed an abscess in his foot and they had to withdraw. I didn't have to imagine how she felt. Our family had been there.

Now only eleven horse-and-rider combinations would compete. Three days. Five competitions. Perhaps it was lack of sleep. Perhaps it was nerves. We felt the mounting pressure.

Steve called after every event. Mark called after every event. After each call, I would relay the information to family and friends who had asked us to keep them informed. On Sunday, August 6, the fourth and final call came from Steve. He held the phone in the air, then talked into it. "Margie is in the number one position. I just wanted you two to hear the applause. That's your daughter they're cheering for!"

The family finally had a chance to celebrate later in the month. Margie had returned to regular competition with runs out to California to keep Perin exercised while he was in quarantine. She was in South Florida for only a couple of days. Eddie, Beth, and Suzi—Matt and Jeff were away at college—joined Irv and me when we met at The King and I in Miami Lakes for dinner. Along with its great Thai and Japanese food, this restaurant—midway between our various distances—had served (over many years) sushi and solace, sizzle and celebration.

As we toasted our successful daughter, I asked, "Margie, we've all been nervous wrecks. How have you stayed so calm?"

"There's so much to *think* about when you're riding."

Suzi looked at Margie thoughtfully. "What do you mean?"

"You have to really be in tune with the horse: aware of what's in his mind, how he's responding, where to speed up, where you have to approach cautiously. The courses for the Olympics Trials are especially tricky."

Now it was Ed's turn to ask, "How so?"

"Not only were the obstacles more difficult—wider oxers, wider water hazards, and flat cups that barely held the rails—but the strides between hurdles were quite complicated. The course designer built half strides added to full ones, so you really had to have good communication with your horse. You're constantly adjusting his stride, lengthening or shortening it."

"But you kept your clothes clean!" I teased.

Margie colored slightly, then looked at each of us. "You *know* I'm not superstitious. Honest!"

I felt mischievous and grinned at one and all as they stared back with no clue to the meaning of this unexpected conversational reference. "I'll bet your family would love to hear about your one little pre-show ritual."

"Okay. Okay. It began with Spank. Whenever I was wearing something new, he'd pick up a little bit of dirt and rub it onto my clean clothes. Then he'd tell me: 'You're going to get dirty the *easy* way or the *hard* way. Let's do it the easy way.' I guess it's just habit now, but I do the same thing for me and for my pupils."

I laughed, then lifted my glass. "Well, it's a nice way to remember Spank. Meanwhile, a toast: We're awfully proud of you—on and off the course! Good luck in Sydney—and you and Steve, enjoy, enjoy!"

Margie left the following morning. We resumed visiting by phone, but the month between the conclusion of the Olympic Trials and leaving for Sydney was hectic. I asked, "Margie, what's going on? Every time we talk to you, you're in another city and winning another Grand Prix."

"Well, I'll be in Sydney for several weeks, and I want to stay in shape. Also, I want to keep the other horses, the ones who weren't in the trials, going. It's way too easy to get rusty."

Irv said, "We're getting phone calls from friends and relatives all over the country who have seen you in delayed broadcasts from the Hamptons or Indianapolis or Port Jervis or Boston. How are you making all these connections?"

The memory of anticipation and excitement accelerated Margie's words as they tumbled out in explanation. "When I told the officials that I couldn't get from the Grand Prix in Port Jervis to the one in Boston just a few hours later, they said they'd send a private plane and a limo for me. We got to the airport and were fogged in. We were late and the show had already started. They let the three of us—Lynn Little, Candice King, and me—walk the course between riders."

I gave her a startled reply. "Good heavens! How do you take that kind of pressure?"

Margie laughed. "I won the top spot and Lynn came in second."

Irv chimed in. "When do you leave for Sydney? How about Perin—when does he fly over?"

"Oh, I spoke to the groom, who flew with Perin. He said that, from the moment they put him in the large container, he didn't like it at all! But if he wasn't left alone, then he was fine."

I exclaimed, "Poor guy. He just wanted company. What happened to him when he landed in Australia?'

"Once they landed, Perin went into quarantine again."

"And what about you and Steve? When do you leave?"

"I'll be leaving for LA in a couple of days—the USET officials will be going over the rules and expectations with the team—and Steve will follow just a few days after that."

Family and friends continued to call. One of the calls that I truly cherished came from Karen Harndon-Smith, Margie's mentor.

"Hi, Mrs. Goldstein. I just wanted to let you know how thrilled we all are about your daughter. I hope you realize how terrific she is."

"Well, Karen, you've just proven why it's so great talking to you. Only kidding—I love to hear from you. I agree, but we're a little biased."

"During Marj-or-ee's last visit . . ."

"You still tease her with that gosh-awful name?"

"And she still hates it! Anyway we had the greatest talk the last time she was here that I wanted to tell you about it."

"How were you both able to meet? She's busier than ever."

"We met at Sherri's—while we were waiting for our hair appointments, we talked and talked and talked—haven't been able to do that in years. I told her that in one way I was kind of sad. She was doing everything I had wanted to and never was able to."

"Oh, Karen . . ."

"No, no, it's all right. Margie reminded me that it was all a matter of choice. 'You've raised three wonderful children—you *chose* to do that,' she said. 'You could have been an Olympian or gone as far as you wanted. You *chose* that path.' Then she went on to ask if I could possibly regret that choice and I couldn't say I did. In fact, after I spoke to her I felt so good that she was doing this for *all* of us at Gladewinds. She's just a fine human being. You should be so proud of her, Mona."

"Karen, surely you must know that a part of *you* is going to Sydney also."

Karen laughed. "Your daughter told me those exact same words."

Another exchange that delighted both Irv and me was an e-mail from Nancy Unger Fink and her ten-year-old daughter. Nikki sent a copy of her school report, an extremely comprehensive biography of Margie that included the early days at Gladewinds Farm, the ponies Margie broke, trained, and showed, her college years, and her professional history. Nikki wrote, "She became somewhat of a phenomenon. . . . She is currently the best rider of show jumping in the history of the United States. . . . Margie is like the president of the country in the horse world. All horse-loving kids look up to Margie as a role model. She is really good at writing to people that write her fan mail." Her last paragraph concluded with Margie's Olympic dreams and hopes.

I answered Nikki that, as a fourth-grade teacher, I would say she'd earned an A+ in every category: sentence structure, vocabulary, punctuation, creativity, organization, and more. When I teased her that the only thing she hadn't included was mention of her mother's and Margie's giggling, she found a way to work that into her report as well.

I'm sure it's no surprise that Nikki's composition received a prominent position in Margie's scrapbook.

The trips for Margie and Steve were equally long and tedious, but from the moment of their arrival, the sense of place and pleasure never left them. Two years earlier, Irv and I encountered only fun-loving, gracious Australians in our travels through their country. The Engles, as guests of the Olympic host country, met (as they told us later) "the most happy, helpful, friendly, and efficient people in the history of the planet. Everyone greeted us with 'G'day' and—when we say everyone—there are thousands and thousands of volunteers who made everything so easy and so delightful for all the Olympians. The merchants gave us magic coins to use in the vending machines. We not only got our selected items, but our coins boomeranged back as well. Their hospitality tents included food for every nationality and it was all free!

Along with the rest of the Olympic equestrians as well as the rowing teams and support personnel, Steve and Margie were housed in a little country town called Penrith to be near to their competitive venues. When they drove into Sydney, twenty-five miles away, they carefully dodged numerous kangaroos on the road. Cute as these unique-to-Australia animals were, they presented a formidable obstacle to the newly arrived visitors who had to navigate around them. (To avoid hitting the 'roos, native Australians drive with special bumpers on their cars.)

Margie and Laura Kraut relaxed with a game of backgammon between classes at the Olympic Games in Sydney. © *Charles Mann Photography*

The day after the inspiring, spirited opening ceremonies, Margie and Steve spoke to an oarsman on the Netherlands team, who told them: "Wow, were we pumped up! We couldn't believe how exciting this would be. We were driving here and—out of the blue—this giant animal appeared in our headlights. We stopped the car and there's this kangaroo—we'd hit him—and we felt bad, but what could we do? My buddy decides he's got to have a picture of this. So he takes off the jacket of his uniform, puts it on the 'roo, and hands me his camera. When I take the picture and the flash goes off, so does the kangaroo. He must have been stunned—now it's our turn. We chase him, but he's too fast for us."

"That's a shame. So he lost his jacket?"

"Not just his jacket. That blasted animal has his passport, his wallet, his credit cards, his Olympic credentials. We'll have to spend tomorrow at the embassy."

Hearing the story, Irv added, "Well, if I see a well-dressed kangaroo in Miami, I'll know he put the passport to good use."

Margie's show-jumping squad had different problems. Steve, who faithfully put his new laptop computer to good use and kept us informed almost daily via e-mail, wrote that despite the team's best efforts, they couldn't reach their expectations. Rhythmical, who was the most experienced horse on the U.S. team, and Nona Garson fell on a slippery course the first day of competition, and they never were able to recover fully. The show jumpers came in sixth in the Nation's Cup, but Margie, as well as Lauren Hough on Clasiko and Laura Kraut on Liberty, qualified for the individual finals.

We enjoyed Steve's e-mail about Margie's excitement in posing with President Clinton's daughter, Chelsea, and meeting tennis superstars Venus and Serena Williams. Most of her days were spent waiting for her turn in the practice ring, but Steve, along with the other spouses, managed to see some of the sights and climb in the Blue Mountains. His days also were filled with various chores; even though he was not the official veterinarian for the U.S. horses, the riders wanted him to keep their horses in tip-top shape, and he happily assisted.

I saved his last two messages, which read as follows:

09/30/2000 7:17:34 AM Eastern Daylight Time

Hi, it's us again,

We went into Sydney last night and had dinner with Mike [Polaski], his entourage, and Jane Clark [owner and official] at a place called "Catalina." It was right on the bay and had great food. When we came out of the restaurant, there were bats flying all about—big bats! We then drove down to Hyde Park where we had a great view of Sydney and the Opera House, which continually changed colors as we watched. There was a laser show so to speak from the tower in town. Sydney was just spectacular at night. The view of the bridge, lit up with the Olympic rings—really beautiful—along with all the glamorous yachts cruising the harbor, made for an unbelievable evening.

We hung at the barn today, because they had to jog this afternoon for tomorrow's event. I was going to go back in to see the track-and-field events tonight, but just ran out of steam.

Big day tomorrow, so it was probably better that I called it a day earlier than I had planned. I'll let you know how things go as soon as I get back tomorrow night. We aren't going to the closing ceremonies—too crowded—so we should be back at a decent hour to get packed. Talk to you soon. We love you all.

S&M

10/1/2000 2:34:33 AM Eastern Daylight Time

It was quite the finish. There were no clean rounds when Margie entered the ring (she was 22nd to go). She rode the course magnificently—over the water, through the combinations, every step rub free but had the last rail down—barely. The crowd roared in anticipation of the clear round and then let out a huge moan as the rail came down. It was a spectacular round. The second round, the wind was really kicking up. I don't know that this contributed to anything, but she ended up with 8 faults giving her a total of 12 leaving her in 10th place. She was leading American (and leading female) rider and we can all be proud of her performance. There were no double clean rounds so there was a 4-way jump off. Rodrigo Pessoa, the Brazilian superstar, was the last to jump and would have to go clean to contend for the gold medal. It was unbelievable—he had the first jump down and then stopped out at the combination. No medal for him. Is this a tough sport or what? In fact, none of those that medaled in the Nation's Cup competition medaled here.

2000   Hidden Creek's Perin, a 17.1-hand Westphalian gelding with tons of scope, a great heart, and a careful nature, is so sweet and loving with people that Margie thinks of him as a big puppy. He had so much ability and power that, despite his lack of experience, he was easy to move up to Grand Prix level. Because he was so laid back, they worked constantly to keep him fit. Also, his large size required shortening his stride. So Perin, like Caribbean Queen, needed much flatwork, work on tight distances and combinations, and no-stride or bounce practice. This picture shows him just before he enters the Olympic arena.
© Charles Mann Photography

This is the last communiqué from Sydney. I hope this kept everybody feeling well informed. We're looking forward to getting home and seeing you all again.

G'day and G'bye from Sydney,

S&M

Overall, the U.S. riders fared well, with bronze medals for eventing and dressage and a record-setting individual gold medal in the three-day event as well. Because of the seventeen-hour difference in time, we knew the results before the events were shown or written about in the United States, thanks to Steve's e-mails.

When Margie called before they left Sydney, we thanked her for providing us with the thrill of a lifetime. "And we're following your advice, honey."

"What advice did I give you?"

"Enjoy the good times. This sport has so many ups and downs, you have to take your pleasure when you can."

When we greeted her on her return, I said, "You must feel so proud, Margie."

She responded. "I was thrilled. The whole thing was just so exciting..." She paused for a deep breath and then continued. "But I can hardly wait until the next time!"

Hidden Creek's Perin showed off his winning form in Sydney. Margie and Perin earned the highest American placement. Margie also was the highest-placed female equestrian.
© Charles Mann Photography

CHAPTER FOURTEEN

Glory Days

"GOODNESS, IRV, WE'RE AN HOUR EARLY and the parking lot is almost full."

As we exited the car on this sunny February afternoon, a white-haired driver called out to us. His white mustache accented his pearly teeth as he beckoned from the almost filled golf cart that welcomed us to the Palm Beach Equestrian Center for the 2001 Winter Circuit. We climbed aboard and greeted our fellow show-jumping enthusiasts. One fan commented, "This cool weather ought to make the horses frisky today."

Our friendly driver agreed. "Yup. Lots of Olympians here today. Should be a good Grand Prix." The ride lasted just a few minutes; we were soon at the entrance.

A shiver of excitement ran up my back as I reached for Irv's extended hand. "Do you realize we'll hear for the first time Margie introduced as an Olympian?" A smile flashed across his face, and I knew he felt it, too.

We walked over to our friends Irv and Adele Kelton, who had driven up from Boynton Beach. We picked up tickets, programs, order-of-go sheets, and staked out our specified tent and chairs.

We watched the passing parade as people popped in and out of the many boutiques and gift shops. Animated groups of families, Pony Club members in either brand-new or well-worn breeches, and everyone from babes in arms to senior citizens ambled by. In their wake, they left lingering aromas of coffee, hamburgers, or gourmet concoctions. Gene Mische,

2001   Cosequin did the honors in the program for Tampa Series, Winter Equestrian Festival, featuring Margie and Perin after their highest-placed American showing at the Olympic Games in Sydney.

president of Stadium Jumping, and Kim Tudor, his able assistant, had set an intriguing stage, and the spectators eagerly anticipated the main event.

Margie and Mike liked to rotate the Hidden Creek Farms horses, so this day she rode Christo. We didn't know him that well, but Margie obviously did, for she won the event and earned the Kilkenny Internationale Cup.

When we met the Engles at the restaurant for a post-horse-show dinner, I complimented Margie on her butter-soft black leather short coat. Five rings on the back were subtly stitched and raised in the instantly recognizable Olympic pattern.

She responded, "Isn't it attractive? All the participants in the Sydney Games received these jackets."

We sat down and she showed it to us. In the lining of the coat, we read the embroidered inspiring sentiment: THE MOST IMPORTANT THING IN THE OLYMPIC GAMES IS NOT TO WIN BUT TO TAKE PART—JUST AS THE MOST IMPORTANT THING IN LIFE IS NOT THE TRIUMPH BUT THE STRUGGLE.

Whenever we meet Margie and Steve after a Sunday-afternoon Grand Prix, there are two constants. First, Margie is always ravenous; and, second, she talks animatedly at a mile-a-minute pace.

After she ordered almost every appetizer on the menu, the conversation began. Our guests asked about the Olympics and how she felt. Slowly and thoughtfully, she responded. "It's hard to put into words, but it will remain something I will always cherish and something I look back upon as a great, absolutely thrilling accomplishment. And because it was such a major event in my life, I'll always have a special bond with the people we shared it with—Laura Kraut, Lauren Hough, Nona Garson, and Todd Minikus."

"And Steve, how do you feel about it?"

"What's not to be thrilled about? The friendly Aussies, the participants—everyone made sure we had the most wonderful experiences possible. While the team waited for their practice time, we husbands explored. We climbed the Blue Mountains. We saw downtown Sydney: the famous Opera House, the harbor, the Harbor Bridge. And everywhere we went, the people could not have been more helpful or accommodating."

I thanked Margie for the wonderful goblets she'd brought back from one of the Olympic sponsors and for a lovely red, white, and blue scarf.

Steve laughed. "I'm glad you have them. Margie has already packed up most of the items from the trials and the games for the Make-A-Wish auction. She sure supports that organization!"

Irv had a question of his own. "Margie, Laura Kraut is giving you lots of good competition for the AGA standings. When does the 2000–2001 year officially end?"

"We'll end in Tampa in April, but I just take it one competition at a time. We have some big shows coming up here in Wellington."

Big shows? Margie faced sixty-eight national and international top equestrians on March 4 in the Tommy Bahama Florida Open Grand Prix. Seventeen riders qualified for the jump-off and gave the viewers an exciting finish. After watching Jeffrey Welles take an early lead with the only clean round at 40.953 aboard Riviera, Margie changed her strategy. "Slow and easy wouldn't do it, so I figured I'd go for it." She and Laurel accepted the challenge and rode a 39.756-second fault-free round. None of the five remaining riders could overtake her lead. Meredith Michaels-Beerbaum of Germany rode her mare Stella to double clean at 40.895 seconds and pushed Jeff Welles to the number three spot.

Margie's big win virtually assured her standing for 2000–2001 AGA Rider of the Year for an unprecedented seventh time and brought her lifetime Grand Prix wins to a total of ninety-five.

As Margie took her victory lap around the field, she spotted us cheering loudly from the tent and gave us a happy wave. I turned to Irv and shook my head in surprise. "Considering how temperamental Laurel is—a real princess who doesn't like being crowded by so many horses—winning this large class is quite an achievement."

Irv answered, "But Margie said once she's on the field and alone, she does her job well, and there's the proof."

In June, Margie, along with other Americans who'd taken part in both the Olympics and the Special Olympics, received an invitation to visit the White House. Afterward, she showed us her picture shaking hands with the president of the United States and related the details. She spoke animatedly, pausing only to take a needed breath. "And I was trying to rush through the receiving line, because there were so *many* of us. But President Clinton held my hand in both of his, gazed at me with those piercing blue eyes—no wonder people talk about how charismatic he is! And the athletes from the Special Olympics—amazing! How they can accomplish so much by concentrating on what they *can* do . . . they're so poised and confident . . . oh, you just had to see them."

About that same time, I self-published the first edition of her biography, *No Hurdle Too High: The Story of Show Jumper Margie Goldstein Engle*, with all profits designated for USET. During the following months, I mailed or delivered copies to various people who had played such a large part in Margie's life. Her mentors and childhood friends from Gladewinds Farm made me feel as if I'd written a best seller.

Sherri Cicero declared, "I feel as if I'm reliving the entire time at Gladewinds."

Bobbi Badgley said, "I loved it and can't believe you remembered all those stories."

Nancy Unger Fink thanked me for the copy I mailed and added, "I've bought fifty more books so I can give everyone at our barn a copy of their own."

Margie's mentor, Karen Harndon-Smith, who had guided Margie's progress so greatly in the early years, laughed at her riding pupils as they gazed at her in awe: "You know Margie Goldstein Engle?"

Since South Miami Elementary School had been so much a part of Margie's early childhood, I planned to donate a book to the school library. I waited for my appointment with the media specialist, then looked at her tense face and knew something was wrong. "Have you heard the news?" she asked. "Terrorists have flown airplanes into the Twin Towers. People are leaping out of the skyscrapers."

I stared in disbelief, but when I left soon afterward, I went home to watch the TV coverage on that horrific September 11. The cruelty and callousness of that vicious attack changed our country forever.

The USET, with understandable concern for the safety of its qualified team (including Margie, Todd Minikus, Beezie Patton [later Madden], and Lauren Hough), canceled the projected trip to the Samsung Nation's Cup Finals in Madrid. Instead, the team designated riders who were currently competing already in Europe: Clare Bronfman, Alice Dabney, and

Clero and Richard Spooner, with Clero Spooner chosen as the chef d'équipe. Back at home, travel, already difficult, became more time consuming for the nomadic horse show competitors.

The early-summer treks of 2001 gave no indication of the changes that were to come after 9/11 or the efforts to maintain a degree of normalcy in the world of show-jumping competition.

In June of that year, Margie broke another record. She became the first rider to win more than one hundred Grand Prix events, thus becoming the most prolific rider in U.S. show-jumping history. Just a year earlier when the twentieth century had faded into memory, Hap Hansen had reigned with a total of eighty Grand Prix wins; Michael Matz was right behind him with seventy-eight victories. Margie also became the first rider to reach $3 million in prize money.

In the first two weeks of July, Margie swept into Lake Placid, winning both of the prestigious top events. With her partner Perin, she first took the Whitney Perpetual Prize Trophy at the July 4 Budweiser Grand Prix (which had been postponed because of rain), then won the I Love New York Grand Prix aboard Reggae on July 7. She joined Leslie Burr Howard and Debbie Dolan as one of only three riders ever to win these back-to-back events.

The jump-off on July 4 presented a unique format and many options for the forty-one riders: Faults were converted to seconds and added to the final time. The long run to the final obstacle brought the spectators to their feet as the eight finalists raced against the clock. Only Margie and Laura Chapot on Sundance Kid galloped to fault-free jump-offs. When McLain Ward on Viktor knocked down one fence, thus adding four seconds, Margie's three-second lead over Laura won the event.

In August, Margie and Steve combined work and play in San Juan Capistrano, California, where they met Mark and Cindy for a few pleasurable days together. It was made even more enjoyable when Margie came in second in the qualifier and, with only four in the jump-off, number one in the Grand Prix. At that time, it was the largest show in the country.

Then the Engles flew to the Hampton Classic in Southampton, New York, a venue known for its luxurious surroundings. Filled with celebrities, this champagne-and-roses event sponsored by jeweler David Yurman

2001   A USET skit at Washington International raised money for the victims of 9/11. Front row: Lauren Hough as a cowgirl, Margie Goldstein Engle as a sailor, Leslie Burr Howard as Uncle Sam; back row: McLain Ward as a motorcycle rider, Lynn Little as a dancing girl. Photographer: *Robin Wyman*

enthralled the equestrians as well as the spectators. Thirty riders who had to qualify during the week for Sunday's Grand Prix on September 2 faced an especially difficult course. Olympic gold medalist Conrad Homfeld knew the competitors and kept their capabilities in mind with his challenging design.

Gasps came from the viewers as all six finalists turned in fault-free efforts. Aboard Rio, McLain Ward—who held the only Hampton back-to-back wins record (on different horses)—went scorching around the seven-fence field in 38.824 seconds and seemed unbeatable. Margie on Hidden Creek's Laurel raced over the hurdles, edging out McLain with a 38.095-second round and winning the Grand Prix for the second year in a row, only the second rider to achieve this distinction.

The Washington, DC, International Horse Show that fall with riders from Ireland, Mexico, Canada, and the United States presented a lighter side to horse show competition with its Pairs Costume Relay Class. A U.S. team dressed as Village People changed the lyrics of their popular "YMCA" song to a patriotic "US of A" rendition and displayed the words on the giant JumboTron for an audience sing-along. They won the Most Humorous Skit Class. Margie emerged as the show's leading jumper and international rider.

"Margie, did you see the news in the 2002 USET publication? The U.S. Olympic Committee has named David O'Conner as the 2001 Male Equestrian Athlete of the Year and *you* as the 2001 Female Equestrian Athlete of the Year."

"I don't know how I missed that."

"Well, I've already pasted the article in your scrapbook, but here's what it says. 'Margie Goldstein Engle spent the entire year as the number-one ranked show-jumping rider on the USET Computer Ranking List leading the ranking all 43 weeks of the competition season.' It mentions your tenth World Cup appearance in 2001 when you came in ninth. The Olympic

In its April 21, 2001, issue, *Sidelines* magazine pictured Margie receiving the 2000–2001 AGA Rider of the Year Award from Frank Chapot. Photograph courtesy of © *Randi Muster Photography*

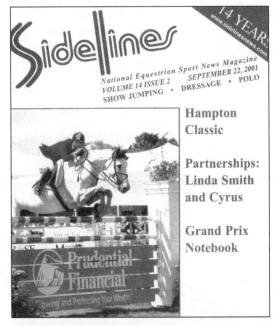

officials were impressed by your double wins in Lake Placid, the back-to-back win in the Hamptons, and they wrote about your beating out a field of twenty-six international entries that included eight Olympians in Culpeper, Virginia. Evidently your twelve Grand Prix wins in 2001 are the most of any U.S. show-jumping rider."

I could almost hear her smile over the telephone.

On September 22, 2001, *Sidelines* magazine featured Margie and Hidden Creek's Laurel winning at the Hampton Classic for the second time. The following year, Margie won for an unprecedented three times in a row. Photograph courtesy of *Classic Communications*

The year 2002 brought a delightful familiarity about Margie's routine. Irv and I traveled to Palm Beach for the Winter Equestrian Festivals with friends and local family. Our oldest son, Mark, his wife, Cindy, and their children traveled to any part of the West, usually Southern California or Las Vegas, to meet Margie and Steve during competitions. When possible, the group took a few extra days just to relax and enjoy one another. Our daughter was healthy, doing well, and the whole family enjoyed her reflected glory.

In fact, somewhere along the way, I had almost lost my anxiety with her riding. I no longer held my breath or squeezed my husband's arm during her breathtaking rounds, but cheered loudly and lustily as she cleared the hurdles. "Go, Margie, go!'

We witnessed her victories on Hidden Creek's Jones in the Bayer Wellington Cup, on Hidden Creek's Perin in the Zada Enterprises Masters Cup, and her team's win at the first Samsung Nation's Cup to be held at an outdoor U.S. site. In addition to Margie and Hidden Creek's Perin,

McLain Ward and Olympic partners Laura Kraut and Lauren Hough—with Kim Frey as alternate—shared in the victory. Margie laughed as she informed us, "This year I could hear you every time I rode."

In April, the only double-clear round of the afternoon resulted in her 108th win at Wellington in the $150,000 AGA Finals aboard her Olympic mount, Hidden Creek's Perin. Pepe Gamarra's tough course included a triple jump set diagonally after a very sharp turn. This obstacle snared two-thirds of the top riders of the 2001–2002 year. Only three of the thirty riders had no faults in the first round, so the top five riders with four faults also competed in the jump-off. For once, Margie slowed down, and with only two time faults she edged out defending champion Schuyler Riley on Ilean who carried over four faults from the original round.

When the Winter Festival was over, both Margie and Steve, whose veterinary, acupuncture, and chiropractic skills kept the horses fit for so many riders on the circuit, headed for a vacation in the Keys before they resumed their hectic schedule.

"Margie, why didn't you tell us that you were one of only fifty-five riders in the world to ever receive an FEI World Cup silver medal?"

"Oh, I thought I told you."

"We read the article in the May *Chronicle of the Horse* that, since its inception in 1979, only

The 2002 *State Line Tack Catalog* honored Margie and Perin with its cover and sponsorship.
Photographer: *Bob Langrish*

riders who have participated in a hundred World Cup competitions received this award. It sure sounds good to us."

We heard in July about her fourth Cleveland Grand Prix win and about her winning Lake Placid's I Love New York Grand Prix for the second year in a row.

When Margie had a couple of days off and she and Steve headed for their home in Wellington, our son Eddie, his wife, Beth, and his daughter, Suzi, as well as Irv and I, met them at our favorite King and I restaurant. We brought interesting clippings that friends had mailed us, and Margie brought me more horse magazines to read and compile for her fourth giant-sized scrapbook.

One of the clippings I brought was from the *Plano Morning News*. In the newspaper's feature story about one of its Texas readers, the reporter had asked his subject to name four guests at her fantasy perfect dinner. Her list read, "Jesus Christ, Elvis Presley, Barbara Bush, and equestrian Margie Goldstein Engle." Now, that's making the big time!

In the middle of a painting class that I audited at the University of Miami, I overheard a young woman talking about her weekend in the Hamptons—and she spoke about Margie. "After being dragged around the field in the morning, she came back in the afternoon to win the class."

That was news to me. When we heard from Margie that evening, she filled in the details. "Don't worry. I'm fine. I'm fine. Yes, Sunday morning, I was riding a young horse and she got spooked. She looked at the jump and kind of fell into it, getting her legs tangled in the poles. When she stood up and ran, my foot was caught in the stirrup. Until my boot came off, I was dragged around the ring."

"Oh, Margie, are you sure you're all right?"

"I won the Grand Prix later in the day—for the third time in a row."

"That's great, but weren't you all shaken up?"

"At the time it happened, it was a little scary. I couldn't get my foot out, but you just have to put such things behind you and concentrate on the class you're doing at the moment."

Would Irv and I ever get used to this sport? When we read about that afternoon at a later date, we realized what a major accomplishment it was to win this Grand Prix, the first qualifier for the 2003 World Cup in Las Vegas. We saw the article in which Margie joked that she'd wanted to be stretched taller by this incident, but we didn't appreciate her humor after reading that she had fallen backward and been dragged for eighty feet. Laurel had won the two previous years. Now Margie and Perin's "three-peat" victory had made Hampton Classic history. It was reported internationally, but we could think of little other than the risks.

A few days later, the USET sent its squad to Calgary for the Spruce Meadow Masters CSIO to compete against Germany, Holland, Switzerland, and the host country Canada, among others. Selected from the Ryegate Computer List of top-ranked riders rather than through qualifiers, the U.S. representatives included Allison Firestone on Casanova, Schuyler Riley on Ilian, and Laura Kraut on Anthem, with Margie and Perin serving in the anchor position. Hailstones, lightning, and thunder alternated with sunshine as only Meredith Michaels-Beerbaum for Germany and both Allison and Margie for the United States turned in the only double-clear rides of the afternoon. The thrilling victory for the American team translated into a Nation's Cup triumph—the first at Spruce Meadows for us in many years.

The horse magazines had already begun advertising for the Washington International Horse Show, and we couldn't help noticing that they were still using the picture of Margie when she rode Daydream at the Puissance competition back in 1986. Evidently, some records are hard to beat.

After leaving the arena in the Washington International Show Grounds, Margie told us about an unexpected visitor. "As I was getting off my horse, I noticed this extremely pretty young woman walking my way— no limp, straight and sure. Her hair was beautiful—full and softly curled. And her children, a boy and girl, gorgeous, looked so healthy. She smiled and said, 'Hi, Margie, remember me?'

"I couldn't believe it! It was Autumn Hendershot. Even after the loss of her leg, she's been completely cancer-free since the last time I saw her almost ten years ago. She told me how much her mother suffered with her other siblings and their bouts of cancer, but I was bowled over when I saw

The Cosequin Winter Equestrian 2002 Festival Program presented a collage of Margie, Joe Fargis, and McLain Ward. Photographer: *James Parker*

how great *she* looked. Then she showed me pictures of her husband and the children. I'm just so happy for her." Margie's radiant face reflected her joy.

After Washington, Margie was leading jumper and foreign rider at the Toronto Royal Winter Fair, one of her favorite shows. Then she returned to the National Horse Show that had moved from the Garden in New York to Wellington for the very first time.

CHAPTER FIFTEEN

New Records

WE NEVER ATTENDED THE JANUARY 26 FIRST GRAND PRIX IN WELLINGTON. In fact, it would be November 2003 before we saw any of Margie's Palm Beach Equestrian events during the year.

I left the message on the Engles' home phone, rather than calling on Margie's cell, so they wouldn't get the news until after the Sunday show. "Margie, Steve—we won't be seeing you today. Don't worry. I think the worst is past, but we spent the night in the emergency room at South Miami Hospital. Dad's now in critical care."

They called immediately and finally tracked me down at the hospital. "No, don't come down yet. Mark wanted to fly in from California, but I've asked him the same thing. I promise to keep you both posted. Dad lost so much blood and that affected his heart. His cardiologist, his gastroenterologist, and the hospital staff doctor are all attending to his care. They're giving him transfusions and monitoring him closely."

Eddie and Beth kept me company in the waiting room; we were allowed into Irv's room for five minutes every hour. Mark's and Margie's calls to the doctors often coincided with our visits. The Engles drove three hours up and back from Wellington so they could see Irv and take me to dinner. After my husband stabilized, the medical team decided they would not remove a portion of his colon but position a coil in the affected area where the diverticuli had burst. Within five weeks, we were back in

145

the ER, and a few days later Dr. Jorge Rabaza performed the emergency surgery.

Recovery took close to eight months, primarily because the long scar from above the navel to the groin exposed the layers of skin that had been cut, and the wound would have to heal from the inside out. Concern drew the family closer. Phone calls and visits became more frequent.

"Margie, bring us up to date with the riding. What's going on?"

"Remember at the beginning of the year I told you that someone offered Mike a lot of money for Hidden Creek's Jones? Well, I want to use Perin sparingly this year so he'll be in good shape for the 2004 Olympics. I promised Mike I'd be selling many of the other horses in his barn so that

In Bud Burgess's montage of Margie and Hidden Creek's Jones at Lake Placid, the pair show why they both were headed for awards at the end of the year. Jones, a 16.3-hand Dutch gelding with mainly Thoroughbred breeding, has lots of blood and energy. Jones is very careful, but a little wiggly with his body, and sometimes he gets behind the bit. So when Margie works him on the flat, she

we could help with expenses, and I can use Jones and many of the new horses that show promise."

"How'd he react?"

"He understood. And he loves the sport, too, so he agreed. Jones is just a top horse even though he's a little harder to ride than Perin. He's sweet, has good jumping technique, is very precise, careful with his front and back end, and uses a very correct style."

As the year progressed, Margie told us about Jones and his big Lake Placid win at I Love New York (the third year in a row for Margie), and his coming in second in the Lake Placid event the first week. "He's living up to all his promise," she told us. "He's leading the AGA standings."

doesn't do too much flexing (he overflexes at the poll), and she works on making him come forward from his hind end and going straight. Jones earned Horse of the Year 2003; in that same year, Margie became an unprecedented eight-time, Rider of the Year. Photographer: *Event Specialists, Inc.*

She also was happy winning at the Grand Prix level with several young horses, including three from Hidden Creek Farms—Charlie Brown, Pasadena, and Wapino—as well as Daybreak Farm's Julius.

"Julius. Daybreak Farm? I don't recognize that name, Margie."

"Yes, you do. Last year I won the Cleveland Grand Prix on Julius. I rode for the owner, Joan Lunden, and her daughter, Jamie Krous, remember?"

She entered the Grand Prix qualifiers for the Nation's Cup, the Pan Am Games, and the World Cup, leading in every one of the events.

Sometime in May, we asked her, "Margie, who are you showing in the Pan Am Games qualifiers?"

"We're all feeling the pressure. If the United States doesn't earn either a gold or silver medal in Santo Domingo, we won't qualify for the Athens Olympic Games next year. Perin, my strongest horse, was in the 2000 Sydney Olympics in his first year doing the Grand Prix circuit. Because this is such an important year, I'll use him."

When the U.S. competitors entered the last two of six rounds at the Kentucky Horse Park trials, two subjective choices had already been made: Chris Kappler and Lauren Hough. Margie on Perin and Laura Kraut on Anthem battled it out with Beezie Patton on Conquest II for the one–two–three positions.

The February 21, 2003, *Chronicle of the Horse* magazine cover featured a stunning colored-pencil drawing by artist Barbara Frake titled *Go Margie!* Publisher: Robert L. Banner Jr.

"Congratulations, honey. It sounds as if there was steep competition. You, Laura, and Beezie competed for your spots on the Pan Am team, but how did Chris and Lauren receive byes?"

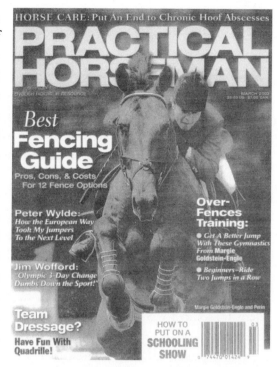

"The selection committee granted Chris a bye after he earned back-to-back victories on Royal Kaliber last month. Lauren had a broken collarbone from a fall in Florida, but had already shown in the first two trials with only one fault. I plan on asking for one of the two subjective spots for the games in Athens."

The March 2003 *Practical Horseman* magazine pictured Margie and Perin on the cover and provided her step-by-step training tips for teaching a horse to improve his jumping through gymnastic exercises. Cover photographer: *Amy Katherine Dragoo* ©

By August, the doctor gave Irv the okay to head for Capistrano and a mini family reunion. Mark, Cindy, Andrew, Ryan, and Caitlin joined Irv and me and stayed at the same hotel as the equestrians. When we joined Margie and Steve for dinners, we presented a lively challenge to any restaurant.

Our youngest family member bubbled over with excitement. "Margie, I think Perin remembered me. Did you see him lick my hair and make it stand on end?"

"Oh, I thought you forgot to brush it, Caitlin." Then seeing the look of mock horror on her niece's face, Margie added, "Perin really does think he's a pet. If he could climb up in your lap, he would."

The adults noted other aspects of the competition. "Joe Fargis sure made us laugh in his post-ride interview."

"Isn't he a great sport? The announcer kept mentioning in both rounds how old he and Edgar were, so he just used that to answer how he felt after winning." In her best Joe impersonation, Margie intoned, "Not bad for an old guy on an old horse."

"Were you Pan Am-bound riders being cautious in the jump-offs?"

"Yes. Our chef d'équipe reminded us that we need everyone in good shape next week. Did you notice Chris didn't even come back for the second round? We've *got* to make gold or silver next week to qualify for the Olympics next year."

With the pressure intensified throughout the hemisphere, the U.S. team headed for the Dominican Republic. They faced a starting field of forty-three riders representing twelve countries. In a hard-fought close competition with Mexico, Margie on Perin, Lauren Hough on Windy City, Chris Kappler on Royal Kaliber, and Beezie Madden on Conquest II (Laura Kraut's Anthem had a slight problem, so the team used Beezie the alternate) secured U.S. eligibility for the Athens Olympics by winning the team gold medal. Chris won the individual silver medal and Margie, the individual bronze as well. Subjective choices, used by most countries worldwide, had proven useful.

With Irv finally able to drive to Wellington, we made up for lost time in late November when we attended the National Horse Show events on Friday night and Sunday afternoon. Margie had used Perin sparingly during the year, hoping to keep him in top form for the 2004 Olympics, so we excitedly anticipated their performance. They didn't disappoint us.

The bright lights of the stadium must have caused shadows that resulted in caution on the part of the riders, because fourteen of the twenty-five riders had time faults in the first round. Only three had otherwise clean rides. In the breathtaking jump-off that followed, Margie took an early lead. Molly Ashe on Lutopia came next with four faults. Norman Dello Joio on Glasgow finished the show and won by fractions of a second less than Margie.

On Sunday, November 30, we cheered even more. Fresh from the awards banquet the previous night, our daughter proved why the AGA had named her Rider of the Year for an unprecedented *eighth* time. Of the eight riders in the jump-off at the Budweiser/AGA Championship, only

Allison Firestone and Margie turned in double-clean rides. Margie's win represented her 125th Grand Prix victory; she also became the first rider ever to win the Championship-CSI event for the third time. One reporter, noting that four of the riders knocked down the last fence, quoted the winning Margie: "Perin's good at galloping, so I wanted to make up some time on the first four or five jumps. I figured if I took a shot at the beginning, I could slow down toward the end. Luckily things worked out as Perin is very careful and great in a big open field."

Wellington was proud of its hometown Olympian and eight-time AGA Rider of the Year. Margie received acknowledgment in the winter 2003 *Wellington Lifestyles* magazine cover and from the city council proclamation of Margie Goldstein Engle Day.
© Shelley Heatley Photography

We attended Saturday's festivities with such a sense of pride. Not only had Margie won Rider of the Year, but she also rode Hidden Creek's Jones to 2003 Horse of the Year. We listened to all the accolades, including one from the mayor of Wellington, Tom Wenham, telling us about the upcoming proclamation of "Margie Goldstein Engle Day" at the next city council meeting. In her acceptance speech, Margie gently teased both herself and the Rookie of the Year, Michael Walton (she does love off-color puns, which caused Michael to turn beet red as she spoke).

Mike Polaski kept the celebration going at a nearby café. It was freezing cold in the breezy outdoors, but I wrapped myself in one of the two heavy horse blankets presented as awards. However, little could spoil the warmth of the evening as we relaxed and reveled in the year just past.

On November 29, 2003, a totally festive mood prevailed at the AGA Awards banquet as Gene Mische, CEO of Stadium Jumping (center), and Alan Balch, president of USA Equestrian (right), made the presentations: Michael Walton as AGA Rookie of the Year, Margie Goldstein Engle as AGA Rider of the Year (for the eighth time), and Mike Polaski accepting the AGA Horse of the Year for Hidden Creek's Jones. Photographer: *Linda Wirtz* ©

CHAPTER SIXTEEN

Bad Breaks

THE GLOW FROM 2003 lingered as Margie and Steve vacationed in Belize with Ray and Lynn Little and their family over the December holidays. Then the Winter Equestrian showjumping circuit began in 2004 with Margie ranked number one on the computer lists. The U.S. Olympic Committee had mailed out its new calendars with Margie and Perin representing the month of October. We had our usual plans with friends to enjoy the Sunday spectacles when the call from our daughter changed everything.

"Mom, Dad, don't worry. I'm in Palms West

Margie admires Mike's commitment to the sport. "He is always looking to do whatever he can to help the horse industry in every capacity." Photography by staff of *Chronicle of the Horse*, February 2004

Hospital. Steve is with me. It was a fluke. We were walking in the warm-up ring, and a horse began to colic and fell on my hip."

Her voice sounded weak and racked with pain, yet she still tried to protect us from her news. Fear and worry clutched my heart. Realizing that we were having trouble accepting what we had heard, Steve took the phone from Margie and assured us that she would receive good medical care. She would need a metal plate, rod, and screws to reposition the broken twisted femur and hip. "Dr. Craig Ferrell, the surgeon from the Olympic Committee, came to see Margie, and he says Dr. Wilbert Piño has an excellent reputation. The operating rooms are all in use so they'll keep Margie sedated, but we have to wait till early tomorrow for the operation. I'll call you after it's over."

We moved robotlike through our days, connected to Margie or Steve through our frequent daily phone calls. "Margie, we can't wait any longer. We want to see for ourselves how you're doing."

"Please wait. I have so much help here at the hospital, and I know I'll need you when I get home."

We couldn't stay away. The accident had occurred on Friday, the thirteenth of February. It was now several days later. Driving on Wellington's South Shore, we passed the turn-off to the Palm Beach Equestrian Center with four billboards advertising the Equestrian Winter Festival. Dominating the display was a large picture of Margie atop Perin. How ironic, and how sad! We dropped our luggage at the Engle home and headed for the hospital.

There was not one spare inch in Margie's room. Flowers were on the windowsills, stands, and floor, with stuffed animals, cards, gift baskets, favorite foods everywhere, along with folks from the horse world visiting. How could so many people fit into one room? We squeezed our way over to the hospital bed to see our daughter. If we didn't know better, we would have thought she was having a party. A laughing and well-medicated Margie compared war wounds with Debbie Stephens and Jimmy and Danielle Torano. Irv and I hugged and thanked Bobbi Badgley and Patti Harnois for their amazing assistance during this emergency. We met Debbie Lane and Peter Lane, gratefully acknowledging his rescue of our daughter.

The accident had happened quickly, with the horse throwing himself to the ground in what was later determined to be colic pain. He had pinned Margie under his seventeen hundred pounds as he thrashed in misery. "I have scratches all over my elbows where I was trying to pull myself from under him, but his weight was just too great," Margie remembered. "The second time he landed on me, I could hear the loud crack of my bone breaking."

Debbie Stephens added, "No one saw it at first, so I steered my horse in front of Margie to keep the other riders from coming too close."

"That's when Peter reacted quickly and pulled the horse off me," Margie said with relief.

Less than a week after the operation, the medical team wanted to transfer Margie to the rehabilitation center, but she opted to set up a hospital bed at home. A visiting nurse dressed her wounds daily, and a physical therapist came three times a week to guide her toward recovery. Her traumatized left hip and leg were immobile, she could not sit up, and the slightest jarring caused spasms of intense pain. Steve brooked no arguments: "You're coming home in an ambulance."

We had gone through accidents with Margie before, but never had we seen her so helpless. And she, never having been through an operation of this magnitude, expected faster recovery than her battered body could accommodate.

There must have been times when Margie felt completely frustrated, but the face she presented to the world was cheerful and upbeat. The constant visitors, the multitude of flowers, lunches, dinners, letters, and calls from acquaintances and friends, past and present, kept her busy and grateful. As she read all the articles reviewing her accomplishments, she commented, "My goodness, I feel like I'm reading my own obituary. Look at this one by Ken Kraus on the Towerheads Web site. He listed all my milestones. He remembered the time in Washington back in 1987 when Daydream and I won the Puissance and tried to break the world high-jumping record. Ken called it his single most exciting moment as a spectator of show jumping."

I had prepared dinners at home to take to Margie and Steve, but instead found that my biggest challenge was to find room in the refrigerator or freezer for all the meals her supportive friends contributed. It's impossible to list everyone, but JoAnn Kovacs, Lynn Little, Bobbi Badgley, Patti Harnois, Genette French, and Lea Allen (to name just a few) made life a lot easier.

I can't say enough about the wonderful equestrians who helped Margie enormously by riding the horses she had already entered for the Wellington events. Beezie Madden, Henri Prudent, and Marilyn Little fulfilled her commitments and relieved her mind. Actually, Margie received more offers of help than she could accept. The riders were top people in every sense of the word.

The battle to get her bones and muscles healed remained her number one priority, and for Margie entire days were spent in therapy of one form or another. "Honey, I heard the therapist tell you to let your body be your guide," I cautioned one day. "You're doing too much."

She stretched the left leg up. "No, no. Just one more time."

"We can see the pain on your face. Go back to your lounger. I'll bring in the heating pads and cold compresses," I said. But her determination—her will to heal and get her body ready for the August Olympics—kept her going.

After two weeks, the caretaker's role had exhausted Irv and me, but we had gained such an insight into the tremendous responsibility involved in running a barn and helping students. Margie was out of competition, but not out of work! She set up her office next to the lounger: a checklist, pencil and paper, two phones (one from the house plus her cell), a laser appliance that she applied at specified times to the wounded area, along with various medications and health supplements.

Every day, Margie and grooms Debbie Lane and Craig Pollard discussed—either over the phone or in person—the condition of each horse: their exercise routine, their feed, or their physical state. Students called to report on show results or to ask for advice or reassurance. Veterinarians, including Jim Kenney and Steve, gave her a daily report on their examinations and carefully planned how to reach the desired goals.

By the third week, Margie could use a wheelchair or crutches. Since she had many pupils in the Wellington horse shows, she rode in a golf cart, propping up her left leg on one crutch as she coached from the sidelines.

Every two weeks, Dr. Piño took X-rays, which he graciously dupli-
cated for Dr. Craig Ferrell, the USOC surgeon; Dr. Mark Brown, who had
treated Margie's back problems a few years prior; and Dr. William Vincent
Burke, a consultant on Dr. Brown's staff. Dr. Piño teased his patient,
"Margie, I feel as if I'm practicing medicine by committee."

"I'm so grateful for your professionalism, as well as your skill," she
replied. "You're so accommodating, knowing there's so much at stake for
me." After each X-ray, Steve took the latest photographs for overnight de-
livery to each of the physicians.

Margie applied to the USET Olympic Selection Committee for a bye
in one of the two subjective team positions. In her application, she included her surgeon's report stating that although she had made remark-
able progress, she would not be ready by mid-May when the trials were
scheduled, but would be ready a month later. "I did remind the committee
that a provisional bye would give them until July 14 for their final decision," she told Irv and me. "If my hip isn't completely healed and they're
not happy with my performance, then the alternate could take my place. I
would gladly drop out if I thought Perin and I would not be in form to be
an asset to the team."

"Of course they'll grant you a bye," I reassured her. "Didn't you tell
us that, in previous years, they've used the procedure of preserving an
Olympic spot for an outstanding injured horse–rider combination?"

"Well, they haven't said yes and they haven't said no. But considering
how well Perin and I performed during the Pan Am Games and his record
of being 100 percent in the ribbons last year, I'm hoping for the best."

We visited the Engles prior to the committee meeting. Margie told us
that many top riders, including Chris Kappler, who already had received
his bye, spoke to individual group members on her behalf. She showed us
Horse International magazine with an article about the approaching
Olympic Trials by Katie Monahan Prudent, a long-respected and prominent Grand Prix rider. Katie, open and outspoken as always, wrote of her
concern for U.S. Olympic results and noted that trial participation could
well scuttle the hopes of the eight-time AGA Rider of the Year. Katie
stated, "Shame on America if the most successful horse-and-rider combination, who would be fit for the team in August, cannot go."

"Well, Margie," I commented, "if Katie held the chef d'équipe position, there's little doubt you'd receive your bye!"

The selection committee met on May 4, after which Margie called us in Miami to report that the committee had turned down her request, saying that she had not shown Perin in 2004. Behind the scenes, however, they advised her that they would do the right thing; they were just keeping their options open. Nevertheless, their decision meant our daughter felt that, even against medical advice, she had no choice but to show them that she and her Olympic horse should be in Athens. From that point on, concern for her physical health overwhelmed all our thoughts.

The newspapers, the wire services, the horse magazines questioned the selectors' denial of a bye. Yet the committee persisted with their unfair-to-everyone plan and met with Margie, Steve, and Mike Polaski, saying "Trust us" right up to two hours before the first Olympic Trial began on May 15 at 7:30 P.M. Compassionate as always, Mike said, "Margie, no one knows how you feel but you. Whatever you decide, I'll support you."

Because her left leg could not carry her full weight and she would have to mount Perin from the wrong side, Margie was lifted onto Perin's back. Steve, Mike, Mark, Cindy, and Margie's niece and nephews in the Del Mar stands held their worry in check as Margie and Perin turned in a flawless round, *leading* the trial by the fastest clear round.

The many phone calls from California to Florida kept us informed about the price she had paid.

"Oh, my God, how badly is Margie hurt, Mark?"

"Dr. Ferrell did not want her to continue. There is internal bleeding and swelling, but he'll take X-rays to make sure there is no further damage to the bone. He'll talk to Margie, Steve, and me later this evening, but he's concerned about more serious injury if she makes any attempt to continue. He gave her medication, prescribing ice packs and rest for now. She and Steve will come back with us to LA for a few days away from all this."

We managed to reach Margie on her cell phone the next day. After checking on her condition, we asked, "The committee could hardly ignore your win last night. What did they say?"

"They told me they were 99 percent sure that I had the second subjective position and they would announce it before the second week of the trials, if possible. I told them that would make whoever came in third or fourth furious. I could understand any complaint those riders might have. If the committee doesn't announce their decision now, they're asking for trouble. They told me the riders would just have to deal with it; they would try to announce it earlier if things played out how they wanted."

"Oh, Margie, what are they thinking? Or aren't they thinking? I read in one of your magazines that Frank Chapot, the chef d'équipe, said you'd be a 'dead duck' if you didn't ride in the trials. You took a terrible risk. You *won*, for heaven's sake. What more do they want?"

"They said they were 99 percent sure I had the position. They just want to keep their options open in case something happened to the horse–rider combination that they wanted on the team. They just kept telling me to have faith in the system."

During the following week, the Engles relaxed at Margie's brother's Hidden Hills home. "Steve and I are feeling so stress-free. I just stretch out in the sun to read around the pool area. We've had individual time with Andrew, Ryan, and Caitlin. Each one is just so special and we marvel at the changes since we last saw them. Caitlin asked us to stay an extra day. She has the lead in her play and, even though the airlines will penalize us, she's worth it."

When they returned to South Florida, we made plans to meet them in "our" restaurant.

"Well, Margie, have you heard from the selection committee?" I asked over the phone.

"Yes, the trials ended last night and they called to tell me they were '99 percent sure' I was going to Athens."

"Great, we'll celebrate when we see you. Thank goodness, that's over."

Eddie, Beth, Irv, and I arrived a few minutes before Margie and Steve. We rushed to greet them as they walked in. "Congra—" We took one look at their faces. "What's happened?"

"It doesn't look good. They're so afraid of being sued—and Mike is so furious and insulted, he's ready to sell the barn and get out of show jumping all together. He's donated millions to support the sport and this is the way they thank him."

"Then why don't you and Mike sue?"

"Mom, I just don't like the idea of suits. The problem is, I know this is the way anyone who competed would feel when the committee handled it the way they did."

Our night of "celebration" was strained. We looked at Suzi and her boyfriend Scott's prom pictures and tried to carry on a conversation about their graduation and college plans.

No one in the Goldstein or Engle family got much sleep that night. I spoke to Margie the next day. "How are you doing, honey?"

"It is what it is. I can't let them make me bitter. If they had taken a strong stand in the beginning and given me a provisional bye, the riders—and I understand how they feel—would have entered the trials with full knowledge of their chances. I believe in my sport and will work on future rules committees to see this never happens to anyone else. It's just plain wrong! I'm calling the Olympic-bound winners to congratulate them and wish them good luck in Athens."

"Margie, you may have been defeated by misleading information, but—as far as I'm concerned—you're surrounded in glory! I love you and am so proud of you. Knowing that you feel that way will make it easier for Dad and me to move on, too."

"The X-rays show that your bone is healing well," the doctor told Margie a month later. "Your soft tissue is what worries me. The muscle, the ligaments need time and therapy to mend."

"But Dr. Piño, you told me five months."

"Margie, can you tell me you won't fall?"

"No one can guarantee that, but this is what I do. I compete."

"Don't forget what I told you. You have so much metal on your bone that if you fall, the stress will cause a break somewhere near the hip injury. At some point, probably eighteen months from your original surgery, we're going to have to take out all the hardware."

Toward the middle of June, Margie started back on the horse show circuit. She showed just two classes the first week and added more as time progressed. Although she still needed assistance getting onto the horses and could not mount them from the correct side, she rode well. By July, she was winning firsts or seconds in every show she rode.

Her good friend Nancy tracked her down by phone. "Hi, Margie. What are you doing up there? We're reading about you on the Internet, and it sounds as if you're winning everything in sight."

"Hi, Nancy. Not quite *everything*, but it feels good to be back."

"Well, I heard you came in first in Cleveland at the HITS show, in Saugerties, New York, and in Lexington, and took second in Lake Placid and Upperville. Plus I heard that the announcer in Upperville gave you quite an introduction. What did he say?"

"At first I was concentrating so hard on the jump-off, I wasn't sure I heard right. He said, 'Now, good people, if you think Margie should be going to Athens, put your hands together and make a lot of noise.' And they sure did."

In fact, many "good people" made their views known through letters to the Engle home, to the horse magazines, and through messages on the *Chronicle of the Horse* Web page. We never did find out the identity of "ponybreath2," although we tried. The following excerpt is from the anonymous posting:

> . . . the Olympics has not much to do with how the horse show world in the USA will ever judge her ability, or her involvement in the sport from the grass roots level to the high end level. She has been a major role model for children and other professionals for many years. She has been a person that inspired so many children to ride, given so much encouragement. . . . I am sad that she will not participate in the games, but her life-long legacy is kindness, and hard work, and coming from nowhere, which everyone says you can't do any more. I am an "R" judge, older than Margie. . . . Bless her. I wish her all the best. . . ."

On this clear August day as they walked the Lexington course, the two riders presented an unusual sight. One was probably the shortest competitor on the field. The other surely was the tallest. Joe Fargis, his long legs thrusting out with ease, said to Margie, "I see you're still having trouble walking. How's the mounting going?"

"Well, I'm still using a ladder and still getting on from the wrong side, but the horses seem to accept it."

When Margie told us how kind Joe always was, I remembered his visit soon after her hip operation. I had opened the front door of the Engle home and immediately recognized his tall, lanky figure. He was dressed all in white and carried a large black leather briefcase. As we sat in the patient's room, Margie and Joe compared their various injuries and operations.

"I asked if you wanted to see my medical 'trophies.' Are you sure?"

Margie reassured him and he reached into his briefcase. Both of us burst out laughing. Joe had pulled out three clear Plexiglas plaques. Each held an artistically arranged display of nuts, rods, and screws. "After my broken parts mended, I had all the metal removed. This came from my ankle. This was in my wrist. And this, with the larger piece in the center, came from my mended hip."

"Joe, did the doctor recommend removal?"

"No, I just couldn't stand the thought of all that foreign material in my body."

Competitions proceeded all over the United States, but riders across the country had their eyes and ears tuned to the equestrian events in Athens. We watched the Olympics on TV, but for us an important rider was missing.

"Margie, glad to hear from you—you're so good about the weekly progress reports. Where are you now?"

"We left Lexington last night and will be headed for Indianapolis tomorrow."

"How did the Kentucky Classic go?"

"I came in first on Perin, second on Wapino, and fourth on Jones in the Grand Prix."

"That's wonderful! Are you feeling all right, though? You're riding a lot of horses again! Well, Margie, what did you think about the Olympic outcome?"

"Beezie did a great job for the team events—all those fault-free rounds! Chris must be thrilled with a team silver and an individual bronze."

"Have you heard how his horse is after he stumbled?"

"It looks as if Royal Kaliber is going to be fine. They were just being doubly careful when they took him to be checked." (Sadly, Royal Kaliber died of colic soon afterward.)

Our conversation took a more immediate turn. "Are you coming back to Wellington before your next venue?"

"Steve will try to make it back. With all these airline cancellations due to Hurricane Charley, I can't take a chance on changing my reservations. We're now watching Frances, and it looks like a big one!"

When the two of them returned to their home at the first opportunity, Palm Beach County had major damage. Steve and Margie fortunately had no serious harm to their home. However, they lost their electrical power and spent their scant time there cleaning up the broken trees and disposing of spoiled food in the refrigerator and freezer.

"We'll have to wait to see you. This is the worst hurricane season either Dad or I can remember." Within the next few weeks, we sweated out Hurricane Ivan; then Hurricane Jeanne came roaring back through the same Palm Beach area.

"What's going on at the shows?" I asked after the hurricane discussion.

"One of the local announcers congratulated me on winning the Grand Prix at the Fidelity Jumper Classic in Boston and asked if that was the first one I had won since returning to competition. I told her, 'No, it's the eleventh.'"*

"Well, Mr. Pergament must be happy. We read about you and Nobility also winning the Turnabout Farm Welcome Stake and that you were the first rider to ever win both classes in the same year at the Fidelity. That makes it your 141st AGA Grand Prix win! It's also enough to bring you up from 125th in June to second in the 2004 AGA standings. Considering you were out of competition for five months, I call that rather amazing!"

"Have I told you about Frances Snodgrass's new horse, Animagus? He rode two clear rounds in yesterday's Capital Challenge Grand Prix in Upper Marlboro, Maryland. I'm so glad for her."

---

*Please see the appendix, Margie's Milestones, for complete listings.

"Frances is such a nice lady. She must have been thrilled. We remember watching the quiet pleasure she got just from watching her horses compete."

"She's in an assisted living home and can't travel, but I'll send her a tape. It was a nice surprise that her horse did so well. Of course, wouldn't you know that I declared for Jones, figuring he was the more experienced of the two horses. Since he had just one clear round, I didn't get as many World Cup points."

Her win on Hidden Creek's Wapino in the Merrill Lynch Cleveland Grand Prix for an unprecedented sixth time placed Margie in the Cleveland record book. She won in 1992, 1997, 1999, 2000, 2003, and now 2004. Additionally, Margie brought along the new horse Animagus for a fourth-place position, beating out the competition in the open jumper

Narem, owned by Shay and Bob Griese, is extremely careful and fast. If you let him get too fast, he got flat, so Margie sometimes added strides in the first round to slow him down physically and mentally. Narem is a real winner.
Courtesy of © Randi Muster Photography

speed stake aboard Shay Griese's Narem, and the welcome stake aboard Robert Pergament's Nobility.

"My top horses all need to stop competing for a while. They've had a busy schedule these last few months. I'm off to Europe for all of next week. We're looking to buy if we can find anything promising."

After the Syracuse show ended on November 7, Margie called, pleased that she had won Friday's event on Animagus and Sunday's Syracuse Cup on Animagus and Nobility.

We read on Towerheads.com about our daughter's win. After a week-long competition in three phases with a requirement of at least two horses, only seven riders qualified to compete for the cup: Margie, Leslie Burr Howard, McLain Ward, Laura Kraut, Kim Frey, Anne Kursinski, and Beezie Madden.

The first phase was a Speed Class with faults converted to time added. Both Margie and Beezie had faultless rounds, with Beezie almost four seconds ahead of Margie. The next phase was a four-bar competition with four rounds. It began with the highest fence at five feet, one inch and ended with the highest fence at six feet, two inches. Beezie had a knockdown during the fourth round but was still slightly ahead of Margie, Laura, and Leslie. The final phase involved time in the first round with faults added to the running score. Margie and Laura turned in the only clear rounds, resulting in Margie's win of the Syracuse Cup, Laura coming in second, and Beezie in third position. To add to the pleasure, Margie had won the Steele Associates Speed Stakes earlier in the week, earning her the Hidden Creek challenge bonus of $10,000.

However, the Grand Prix win was a bittersweet victory. Margie spoke to the owner Frances Snodgrass's daughter and learned that Mrs. Snodgrass had died that very day. "She didn't get to see the tape, but her daughter told me that the only time she perked up at the end was when they told her about Animagus." Fittingly, this lovely, gracious lady left life as a winner.

We attended the December 21 National Horse Show in Wellington. When the announcer introduced Margie, his voice rang out: "Margie is the first rider to reach $4 million in prize money. Her Grand Prix win on Charlie Brown earlier this week brings her 2004 total to fifteen wins and a career total of 142."

* * *

In a year of great difficulty, Margie returned to doing what she loved. Sometimes when we watch her limping, we recoil at the career she has chosen. Yet we remind ourselves: How many people rejoice in their work? How many delight in days of fulfillment—challenged at all times to top performance?

Irv and I look at our daughter. We know about all the obstacles. We know about all the injuries, past and present. Even now, when she's at the top of her field, the risks are always there. We know how hard it was for her when she was growing up with no horse of her own, working in the kennels for extra lessons. We watched her find extra time, planning and juggling her schedule when other priorities made her riding dreams seem impossible. We know how difficult it was to be a catch rider when she was trying to work her way up to the A circuit, willing to try *any* horse just for the opportunity to compete. We knew exactly how she felt when professionals tried to dissuade her from show jumping because of her small stature and lack of financial backing. We worried about her the entire time she was a staff of one, driving a truck down mountains that made sure the weight of the horse trailers behind her pushed them to unwanted speeds.

Yes, there were many obstacles—on and off the course. But for Margie Goldstein Engle, no hurdle was too high!

CHAPTER SEVENTEEN

A Clinic with Margie

WHEN MARGIE IS NOT COMPETING, she spends as much time as she can conducting clinics around the country. She enjoys teaching and the energy she gets from her enthusiastic students. And her students appreciate her thoughtful analysis and encouraging approach, which is why her clinics are always filled.

In clinics, you have different levels of rider experience, everything from beginner riders and pony riders to experienced people on green horses. In this case, they would all use the same lower heights (one to two feet) for jumping. Margie prefers to have at most between four and six in a session. Sometimes sessions have up to eight, but usually it's hard to give too much individual attention if you have so many people.

Here's what Margie has to say about how she conducts her clinics and how her pupils can get the most from them:

"Let's begin with the basics. When students come to a clinic, they should show up wearing the proper clothing and bringing the right equipment. Riders should wear riding boots, breeches, gloves, a hunt cap, spurs, and (unless their horse is very sensitive and afraid) a crop. Apparel should be clean.

"The same thing is true of the horse's equipment. It shows you're more interested when you and your horse are properly turned out for whatever division you're in—hunter or jumper class—everything should be clean and polished. You should be responsible for your horse's equipment and your own equipment.

"If possible, you should try to read books by top trainers, such as *Horse Seat Equitation* by George Morris and *Riding and Jumping* or *The Complete Book of Show Jumping* by William Steinkraus, to name just a few. Such books familiarize you with various terms and the sport's language in general. You'll be that much farther ahead.

"Also, ask questions. I tell the clinic students, if you don't understand or you want to learn about a specific aspect, don't be afraid of asking. Don't interrupt—but that's how you learn. You watch, listen, and ask.

"Flatwork is extremely important; that's probably 90 to 95 percent of what we do with the horses between the shows. The better the horse goes on flat, the more ridable he is over fences. The less you jump, the better it is for the horses. Mentally, it keeps them more alert if they don't overdo. There's less chance of their being injured. You want to do only enough jumping so they stay fit and are using their jumping muscles. Flatwork also provides the students an opportunity to work on their distance and position.

"First, I introduce the riders to the different aids. The rider's hands, through the use of reins, signal or steer the front end and ask the horse to slow down. The rider's legs steer the back end and also keep the horse's 'engine' running behind.

"We begin with the rein aids: the direct rein, pulling straight back; the right indirect rein, right hand toward your left hip; the left indirect rein, left hand toward the right hip across the horse's withers; the bearing rein (which is like a neck rein—lean the rein on the horse's neck); and the opening rein, holding your hand out to the side. This is just a brief introduction, and if there are questions, I explain in more detail. I want everyone to have the same jargon or wording. If a rider does not understand the purpose of each rein, I explain the circumstances when each would be helpful and encourage questions.

"If a horse is cutting in on a turn or leaning in with his shoulder, I sometimes use an indirect rein in combination with my leg on the side he's cutting into. The bearing rein, sometimes called a type of neck rein, is used with my outside leg if a horse is bulging to the outside.

"An opening rein or leading rein is used to provide your horse a better sense of direction. If your horse drifts right over a fence, you use an opening left rein and right leg to keep him straight without inhibiting his top line over the jump. The direct rein is used when horses are going around the turns and steering normally.

"We start off on the flat at the walk to see how well the horse is responding to his rider's leg aids. We do leg yields first by moving the horse off the rider's left leg, then off the right, staying parallel to the rail and moving the horses off the inside leg toward the railing. At the same time, we try to stay parallel with the rail, which teaches a horse to cross the inside leg over the outside leg and move away from the rider's leg. This is teaching your horse to move away from your leg to yield. When we complete the leg yields, we do shoulders-in, just at the walk and, for more advanced riders, at the trot.

"You want your horses responsive on the flat, teaching both lengthening and shortening stride, going on the bit, moving off your leg. We also work on collection at a sitting trot, teaching your horse to come up from behind but very collected with a shortened stride, then lengthening it. At all three gaits (walk, trot, and canter), you work on the same things: lengthening and shortening, collected sitting trot, regular posting trot, extending trot, all the while getting the horse responsive. You do the same thing at a canter, so that these things come naturally when you ride a course and your horse lengthens or shortens when he needs to do so.

"A lot of what we do when we're working on the flat is lengthening, shortening, and getting your horse supple, especially at the trot and at the canter. When you collect your horse, you still want to keep plenty of impulsion. You want him to shorten his stride, but keep his hind end animated so that it's still carrying him forward and balanced. You want to feel him come up in his back, light off his front end, and carrying most of his weight from behind. The same thing when he lengthens; you don't want your horse to just fall forward and throw himself as a race horse does, because being too much on his front end makes it hard to rebalance for the jump. That's why lengthening and shortening should come from the back end.

"A good exercise to work on collecting and/or extending your horse's stride uses two poles on the ground for a reference point. You first canter the two rails at a comfortable pace and count how many strides you do in between. Next, practice adding a stride by using your legs to generate impulsion while your hands contain the horse. Last, you can leave out a stride by adding more leg and less hand. You and your horse should be comfortable before you try this over fences.

"The main idea when you're jumping is to keep the horse well balanced. The better the horse's balance and the better he gets to the obstacle, the better his jump will be. However, you can still be successful from different distances as long as his balance is correct. His power comes from his hind end, so good balance will translate into a successful jump.

"During flatwork, I also review the riders' position. How they sit makes them more effective. Heels down, eyes ahead looking where they're going, hands in the correct position not only look right, but also serve a purpose. Every rider has a different style, different faults, and different tendencies. When I'm conducting a clinic, I work on weak points or improving whatever needs correcting for each horse and rider.

"Working in a two-point where riders can carry their weight in their legs is useful. Riders should not have to support themselves by their hands, but they're independent of the horse's mouth by being able to support and balance themselves with their legs.

"Once we get through the flatwork and the horses are responsive, warmed up, and loosened up, we start jumping by working through a little gymnastics. We use striding, placement poles, and guide rails to make the exercises simple and properly implemented. Gymnastics improve the horse's natural jumping style, because you can set distances that are comfortable for the horse and rider. You can then concentrate on your own riding position and form. I usually set gymnastic combinations with a trot rail coming in, so riders don't have to worry about seeing a distance. The ground rail positions the horse in the correct distance. Once he gets in, the distances are very comfortable. It's a good way to work on basics for both horse and rider.

"In the basic gymnastic, you start with a low cross-rail (about a foot high in the middle), with placement rails seven feet from both the approach and the landing side. You will be able to trot it both ways. Also, set ground lines on both sides of the cross-rail. If your horse is green and needs to develop depth perception, set the ground lines just out enough to give him a nice takeoff spot. If he tends to be 'drapey' and slow with his front end, roll them out a little.

"When you change the cross-rail to a low vertical, approximately eighteen inches high, you also move the placement rails out about a foot. You are showing the horse that you want him to land inside the placement rail and not on it or beyond. Each time you raise the vertical, roll the placement rail out an equal amount, but no farther than nine feet.

"Your ground lines can be adjusted as well. If your horse jumps past his arc, you can tighten the placement poles to help to keep the center of his arc in the middle of the jump.

"When you ride up to the gymnastic, approach toward the center of the cross-rail in a quiet posting trot. The horse is light in front and carrying himself from the hind end. As he steps over the placement rail, give a crest release. If you feel him backing off a little, give him a little more leg. If you feel him getting too quick, relax your body, stay a bit behind the motion, and do everything in slow motion. As you trot over the fence, leave his mouth alone. If you must do something because he's weaving or going to one corner, use more leg and the least possible amount of rein— just enough to steer.

"Let the horse and the gymnastic do their job. It may feel awkward at first, but the horse learns he has to figure it out. As you practice, he learns to use the ground rail and placement rails to center his arc. He learns to use the distance between the cross-rail or the vertical to look ahead at the placement rail, so he can shorten and back himself up.

"Another gymnastic I like to use is the 'bounce,' or no stride. Once again, the setup is going to guide the horse to perform as expected. We begin with two low verticals nine to ten feet apart. They're set low to reduce the stress of landing. They still do a great job of building muscles, getting your horse sharp, increasing his agility, and keeping his interest. The division of the horse and rider will determine the height of the vertical we use. For a hunter, we'll use one no higher than two to two and a half feet high. With a jumper, we'll go as high as three feet or possibly more, but we generally keep the height to a minimum.

"If a horse has never done a bounce before, I slant the rails so the jumps are more inviting. We alternate the slant, so the horse still thinks 'straight.' For example, the first rail has the right side dropped. The next rail has the left side dropped. When we add a third vertical nine to ten feet away for two bounces, we go back to dropping the right side. Ground lines are on the sides of each jump. Placement rails are about eight to nine feet on the takeoff and landing areas. You can add more bounces with more experienced horse–rider combinations.

"Horse and rider approach in a quiet trot with light contact and impulsion from behind. Again, the gymnastic should do the work for you. As your horse steps over the placement rail, you give a light release. When the horse sees the vertical, he rocks back and jumps off his hind end. By staying off his back, you allow the horse to follow through with his hind end.

"Make sure you don't get thrown back in the saddle. You may even have to grab his mane, to avoid the negative reinforcement of hitting him in the mouth or back. Allow total freedom for his head and neck, using the jump (not your hand) to back him up. After the second vertical, the horse sees the placement rail, brings his hind end up and under, so he can now lift and round over the rail. The rider has stayed off his back and let the exercise do the work.

"The same principles apply with the vertical-to-oxer gymnastic. The vertical is low; eighteen feet away is a two-and-a-half-foot-high, eighteen-to twenty-four-inch-wide oxer. A ground line is placed around six inches in front of the vertical. It is placed directly beneath the oxer. Put placement rails seven or eight feet in front of the vertical and nine to ten feet out from the landing side of the vertical or oxer out of the gymnastic.

"Arrange a chute of guide rails along both sides of the gymnastic between the two jumps. If your horse is young, the guide rails will help to keep him focused and going straight.

"The gymnastic has many variations to correct different flaws. For example, if the horse is slow with his front end, roll out the ground lines six to twelve inches to encourage him to rock back. This gives his front end time to be in the proper position. If he still gets too deep, roll them out even more. If he's young, green, or very slow with his front end, a flower box in front of the oxer can also help him gauge the distance. If he's more experienced, put the flower box *under* the oxer.

"If he jumps past his arc, roll the landing placement rail slightly in, just enough so it helps to back him up and keep his arc centered. If he lands shallow, roll the landing placement rail a few inches out to help him open up and land farther out. If he wants to drift toward one chute rail, straighten him with a little opening rein on the opposite side. If he anticipates the turn after landing and drifts to the inside, move him off your leg (the one on the side he's drifting) to straighten him and make him 'give' on that shoulder. Basically, work on your horse's weak points.

"If we have a more advanced group, after we finish doing the flatwork and gymnastic exercises, we work on lines. For example, I set up a six-stride line and work on it both on the normal comfortable distance in six strides, then teach the riders to be comfortable lengthening the stride so they cover the distance in five strides by leaving out a stride. You want to make each stride the same and let the horses learn to lengthen from where they land.

"Then we shorten the stride and try to take seven strides so horses and riders become comfortable with shortening. You want horse and rider adjustable. When you jump into a line, you can either go forward or have your horse wait for you and shorten his stride when you want. My goal is to teach your eye to be adjustable and the horse to be responsive, adjustable, and comfortable at both waiting and going forward.

"As a participant in a clinic, you should always pay attention to problems other riders are having and how to solve them. It may be something that will come up later in your riding, either with a different horse or on a different day. You can learn from other riders' mistakes or from what they're doing correctly. You should learn to listen to what advice is given to you individually and to the other students. You can learn from almost any situation.

"There are different levels of riders, anything from beginners on up to the advanced level, so I tailor the clinic accordingly. The heights are different, but ordinarily I don't have the jumps that high. Normally it's just working on basics and trying to improve rider position. It's not how high the horse can jump. It's just working on doing things correctly."

"In addition to giving advice at clinics, I receive many letters from people asking questions. I remind them that it takes years and years to build a

The Vertical-to-Oxer Gymnastic

Margie first practiced trotting figure eight over the front placement rail, then worked with basic and bounce gymnastic exercises. In the photo above, the bounces have made Savannah think about rocking back on her hind end. For this little vertical, she's rocked back hard and is studying the oxer in photo 2, looking for what she needs to do to come out.

Savannah has opened up on her stride nicely after judging that she had more room. She learned from the bounces where she had to shorten her strides. She landed very balanced, hind legs deep under her, so she easily was able to lengthen her stride and stretch out her head and neck. She's figured out what to do over the oxer. Since the horse has seen chute rails before, Margie angles them in more toward the oxer than she would for a horse who's never seen them. With the rails in place, Margie doesn't need to use an opening rein.

Note the beautifully centered arc. Savannah pushed off well behind without getting flat. For this size fence, she's round over her back and through her head and neck, very even with front and hind legs, and watching the landing rail. Margie stays off her back and lets her jump close her angle.

Savannah tucks up very tight and even behind as she lands, stretching out her head and neck for a neat ending. She lands right between the oxer and placement rail, keeping the oxer in the center of her arc, not cutting down or landing out past the jump, looking at the rail and where to continue when she lands. Margie stresses not interfering and staying off your horse's back.

Photographer: *Mandy Lorraine*

horse's confidence, ridability, and technique. You start by doing flatwork, basic gymnastics, and cavaletti ('small horse' or 'saw horse'—close to the ground) work, and each horse—depending on his age and temperament—learns at a different rate. It's safer to go slowly, like a child learning at elementary school.

"The questions they ask include everything from 'How did you get where you are?' to 'How do you get started?'—many people ask that—to questions about the different horses I ride, such as 'What is Perin like?' or 'What is Jones like?' They ask, 'If you don't have a lot of financial backing, how do you get where you are?' 'What does it take to become a good rider?' 'What does it take to become a Grand Prix rider?'

"I also receive lots of letters from riders with horses who have a particular problem—one who rushes the jumps, one who gets very quick after the jump, one who's a stopper, one who cross-canters.

"The question about their horses stopping or refusing a fence comes up often. An older horse who now stops usually has lost his confidence, or something may be bothering him physically. I usually drop the horses down a division or two to a level where they can compete with ease. If there are options in a jump-off, I will take the easier one. For example, going around an obstacle is less difficult than taking the inside turn. Always try to build his confidence by taking the easier option. If it is physical, I get a vet to check him out.

"A young horse who gets spooky at the jump normally needs more experience. Sometimes a junior or an amateur horse has gotten scared and begins to stop. It's a good idea to get a professional to ride your horse for a while until his confidence is restored.With young horses who refuse, I start over very small obstacles and build as they start to feel secure. Whatever level they were jumping, I drop two to three divisions down.

With green or young horses, I tell the riders how important it is to familiarize them with the area where they will be jumping. If possible, try to hack in this area so that your horse is not startled by anything new as he goes around the ring.

"Take your time, don't get ahead of the motion, and don't be rushed. If the horse starts to slow down in front of the fence or drop behind you, don't make any big moves. This will only startle your horse and make him worry more. Keep your pace consistent to the jumps by keeping strong leg without throwing your body weight ahead of your horse. This will set him off balance.

"If none of the above works or if your horse is too green, get a professional rider to help.

"Most of the questions are from children who want to know how to become a good rider. My answer is that riding and training are like anything else in life. It's a lot of hard work! If you want to do something well, you have to work at it and try not to get disappointed. Where there's a will, there's a way. Even though it's hard not to experience disappointment, this is a sport with a lot of ups and downs, and you have to learn from your mistakes. It's not just you working as yourself, an individual. It's a sport in which one plus one equal *one*!

"You and your horse—the two of you work together. You're a team, a unit. It's a matter of communicating with the horse and developing horse sense. The more time you spend around the horses and the more time you spend on their backs and on the ground, the more intuition you gain, the more horse sense you develop. To be a good rider, you really need to know a lot about the horses you ride and truly love them.

"Becoming a good rider is not just taking lessons. It's not just showing up at horse shows. It's the way you learn to communicate with horses. It's spending the time with them on the ground, knowing them inside and out.

"It's also important to know about your horses clinically—how they feel on certain days. You want your vet to be the primary caregiver for health issues, but you want to know if something is bothering your horse. You want to notice if there's some inflammation on a certain part of his leg, or a rash or bumps, or soreness that you can pick up at an early stage before it turns into something serious. You should know your horse well enough, and go over him often enough, so you know if he has an inflamed tendon or suspensory or some other soreness or unsoundness. If you want to become a horseman rather than just a rider, you should learn how to spot some of these things. Talk to your vet and have him explain what he looks for and what you can learn.

"You should also know about a proper feeding program and how to use different equipment to keep your horses comfortable, such as ultrasound, magnetic blankets, and lasers, if possible. This is not necessary for every level.

"Let me just say it takes a lot of hard work, and a lot of learning from your mistakes. You take your mistakes, but go on. Riding is a sport no one ever masters. I don't care who they are, how well they do, or how many gold medals they win. We're always learning something from our horses. They're always teaching us something different. You're always riding a new horse with a new problem. That's what makes it interesting.

"That's what is part of the challenge. Riding is not the same every day. Each horse has his own life, his own feelings, his own personality. Learning to recognize each horse's traits is something you have to constantly work on. You try to improve as a rider and horseman your entire life.

"If you don't have enough financial funding to take a lot of lessons or to own your own horse, you have to learn from everything you can. If you really want to learn and be involved in the sport, you have to do willingly everything from cleaning stalls and grooming to working around the barns, as a working student—anything you can do to be around horses.

"If you don't have enough money to ride in a top stable, maybe you can get in touch with a trainer you admire and work for him or work in a barn where you can be around top riders and trainers and learn from them.

"I did everything—helping at every level in a dog and cat kennel, and being a working student—to earn extra money for rides or extra lessons. I went to some horse shows to groom, even grooming for free just so I could be around top horsemen and trainers and learn from them. As a teenager, I went to the bigger shows and groomed, sold programs, or cleaned stalls to pay for my hotels and food—and I was thrilled to be there. When I finished my work, I learned just by watching top riders and listening to what they told their students. I watched riders in the ring and saw which things worked with each horse. I noticed everything, from the care of the horses back at the barn to how riders schooled their horses before the classes. You learn more than you think just being around top trainers and riders.

"You have to be willing to do whatever needs to be done. You can't think you'll start at the top. It's only a few years ago that I got top horses to ride. In the beginning of my career, I rode horses no one else wanted. When you're starting off, you take what you can get. I was offered horses who were stoppers, or were too difficult, or those no one else wanted to ride. Then once the horse started to do well and people saw that I could bring along a horse, I started to get better horses to ride just by word of mouth or by people watching.

"It takes a while. Like anything in life, you have to have a lot of luck. It's not so surprising that the harder you work at it, the more luck you have!"

Appendix: Margie's Milestones

1986

- Margie wins first Grand Prix (in Cincinnati on Daydream).
- Leading Rider at Madison Square Garden (open jumper division) with Daydream and Spindletop USA.
- Three Grand Prix wins.

1987

- Three Grand Prix wins.

1988

- Margie's first World Cup competition in Göteborg (places fourth in Grand Prix at World Cup).
- Two Grand Prix wins.

1989

- AGA Rider of the Year for the first time.
- Saluut II wins AHSA Horse of Year.
- Leading Rider, American Gold Cup, and American Jumping Derby.
- Four Grand Prix wins.

1990

- While still using crutches off the course, wins five top-three ribbons in Grand Prix events.
- Margie and Daydream win Washington International Puissance (third time), Madison Square Garden Puissance, and Toronto Puissance.
- Three Grand Prix wins.

1991

- Six Grand Prix wins plus numerous placements.
- Places four horses in a single Grand Prix competition.
- Wins Attitash Equine Festival for the second year in a row.
- AGA Rider of the Year for the second time.
- AHSA/Hertz Rider of the Year.

1992

- Rides with brace (three broken ribs, five crushed ribs)—wins Rolex/National.
- GrandPrix (NGL) Rider of the Year.
- Places four horses in a single Grand Prix event.
- Four Grand Prix wins.

1993

- Rolex/NGL Rider of the Year.
- First rider ever to place first, second, third, fourth, and fifth in a single Grand Prix class (Rolex Music City, in Nashville, Tennessee).
- Five Grand Prix wins.

1994

- Most AGA wins (five) with the same horse in the same season (Saluut II).
- Most Grand Prix wins (eight) with the same horse (Saluut II) in the same season.
- Most Grand Prix wins (thirteen) in a single season (Tampa Grand Prix, WEF Challenge Series Final in Florida, Music City Grand Prix in Tennessee, Las Colinas Grand Prix in Texas, Germantown Grand Prix in Pennsylvania, Upperville Jumper Classic in Virginia, Town & Country Motor City in Michigan, North American Grand Prix of Detroit, Miller's Harness Company in New York, Vermont Summer Grand Prix, Turfway Park Grand Prix of Kentucky, Columbia Classic Benefit of Maryland, Grand Prix of Delaware).
- Wins World Cup Class in Port Jervis, New York—$100,000 Grand Prix.

- Two Grand Prix wins in two days (Germantown and Upperville).
- First rider to place six horses in the ribbons in a single Grand Prix Class (Detroit).
- Margie's total wins place her in the Millionaires' Club (along with Tim Grubb, Hap Hansen, Rodney Jenkins, Leslie Lenehan, Michael Matz, and Katie Monahan Prudent).
- AGA Rider of the Year for the third time (only Katie Monahan Prudent has been Rider of the Year three times).

1995

- Wins Motor City Grand Prix for the second year in a row.
- Wins Music City Grand Prix for third year in a row on the same horse (Sabantianni).
- Only rider to place five horses in a single Grand Prix.
- Seven Grand Prix wins.
- AGA Rider of the Year for an unprecedented fourth time.

1996

- Six Grand Prix wins.
- AGA/Budweiser Rider of the Year for an unprecedented fifth time.
- Volvo World Cup.

1997

- Seven Grand Prix wins.
- USET team: Nation's Cup winner, Rome.
- USET team: Nation's Cup winner, St. Gallen, Switzerland.
- Leading International Rider in St. Gallen, Switzerland.
- USET team: Nation's Cup second place, Aachen, Germany.
- Leading Lady Rider in Aachen, Germany.
- Individual Grand Prix winner in Rome aboard Hidden Creek's Laurel.
- Individual Grand Prix winner in Arnhem, Netherlands, on Hidden Creek's Alvaretto.

1998

- Nine Grand Prix wins, including $100,000 Rolex/USET Show Jumping Championship at the Bayer/USET Festival of Champions on Hidden Creek's Glory.
- USET team: Nation's Cup Winner, Madison Square Garden, on Hidden Creek's Alvaretto.
- USET team: Nation's Cup Winner, Montreal, on Hidden Creek's Laurel.
- World Cup Finals in Helsinki, Finland—second place.

1999

- Eleven Grand Prix wins.
- USET team silver medal award, Pan Am Games, in Winnipeg, Canada, while riding Hidden Creek's Alvaretto.
- Fulfills lifelong dream: wins American Invitational Grand Prix for the first time.
- Leading AGA computer list for number of wins (Rider of the Year Award for an unprecedented sixth time).

2000

- USET representative at World Cup.
- Fifth-time World Cup finalist.
- Leads U.S. Olympic Trials.
- Highest-ranking American in Olympic Games in Sydney, Australia; highest-ranking female (tenth in individual show jumping on Hidden Creek's Perin, sixth in team competition with Margie providing the only clear round for the United States).
- Ninety-three Grand Prix career wins to date (thereby becoming the first show-jumping rider to win $3 million in prize money).
- All-time leading money winner in United States.
- Most Grand Prix wins in U.S. rider history.

2001

- Seventh-time AGA Rider of the Year (2000–2001).
- Third rider in history to sweep two AGA Grand Prix events at Lake Placid/I Love New York horse shows (riding Hidden Creek's Perin in one event, Reggae in another).
- Cosequin U.S. Grand Prix Invitational Finals in Culpeper, Virginia, winner.
- Hampton Classic Horse Show in Bridgehampton, New York, winner for second year in a row, riding Hidden Creek's Laurel.
- Hidden Creek's Perin wins USA Equestrian Horse of the Year (2001).
- In recognition of her impressive Grand Prix victories, including twelve wins in 2001, the most of any U.S. show jumping rider, the U.S. Olympic Committee names Margie Female Equestrian Athlete of the Year for 2001.

2002

- First rider ever to win Hampton Classic (Prudential Financial) Grand Prix for three consecutive years, riding Hidden Creek's Perin.
- Additional wins earn her 108th career Grand Prix victory.
- Samson Nation's Cup (Spruce Meadows, presented by Canadian National) team first.
- Margie rides Hidden Creek's Perin to USA Equestrian Horse of the Year for second year in a row.

2003

- Team wins Nation's Cup (Canadian National).
- At Pan Am Games in Dominican Republic, Margie and Hidden Creek's Perin win individual bronze medal and team gold, enabling the United States to qualify for the 2004 Olympics in Athens.
- At Nation's Cup 2003 in Wellington, Florida, Margie and Hidden Creek's Jones ride the anchor spot, helping the U.S. team to win with double-clear rounds.

- In Wellington, Forida, Margie and Perin win the leading open jumper title at National Horse Show.
- By year's end, Margie wins 125 Grand Prix.
- Margie rides Hidden Creek's Jones to AGA Horse of the Year.
- Margie earns her eighth AGA Rider of the Year Award.

2004

- Fifteen Grand Prix wins (first Olympic Trial in Del Mar, May, Hidden Creek's Perin; HITS in Saugerties, June, Hidden Creek's Wapino; Lexington Country Air, June, Wapino; Lexington, July, Wapino; Cleveland, July, Wapino; Kentucky Classic, August, Perin; Trader's Point, August, Nobility; Culpeper, August, Wapino; Culpeper, August, Animagus; Boston Speed Class, September, Hidden Creek's Charlie Brown; Fidelity Jumper Classic, September, Nobility; Turnabout Farm, October, Welcome Stake, Nobility; Open Jumper Speed Class, October, Nobility; Steele Associates Grand Prix, Syracuse, November, Animagus; Four-Bar Syracuse Cup, November, Nobility; Table A Class Syracuse Cup, November, Animagus; Chesapeake Petroleum National Speed Classic in Wellington, December, Charlie Brown). Additionally, Margie earned many second- and third-place wins.
- Margie maintains her American Grand Prix Association all-time leader status. Her Grand Prix wins total 142! (Forty-two are AGA wins.)
- Margie is the first rider to reach $4 million in prize money. Her owners must be happy!

Directory of Contact Information

EQUINE PHOTOGRAPHERS:

Cheryl Bender
1715 Shoreside Circle
Wellington, FL 33414
Phone: (561) 784-7046
E-mail: cbender729@yahoo.com

Benson Photography + Sumerset Sport Art
Photography, Design, Marketing for the Equestrian World
Ocala, FL
Phone: (352) 598-0824

Arnd Bronkhorst Photography
P.O. Box 53
3886 ZH Garderen
Netherlands
Phone: **31 577 462929
Fax: **31 577 463294
E-mail: info@arnd.nl
www.arnd.nl

Judith S. Buck
Darkroom on Wheels
4776 Sabre Lane
Manlius, NY 13104
Phone: (315) 682-2269
Fax: (315) 682-4864
E-mail: jbpix@twcny.rr.com
www.darkroomonwheels.com

Bud Burgess
Event Specialists, Inc.
Phone: (978) 649-7186
E-mail: ESIGOLF2@CHARTER.NEW

Al Cook Photography
Phone: (804) 543-6228
E-mail: studio@acphotovideo.com

Amy Katherine Dragoo
1826 Olive Street
Coatesville, PA 19320
Phone: (610) 383-5623
Cell: (610) 656-0258
E-mail: akdragoophoto@comcast.net
www.AKDragooPhoto.com

Crowell Hadden, Jr.
P.O. Box 1766
Middleberg, VA 20118
Phone: (540) 837-1876
Cell: (540) 532-2075
E-mail: Haddenjrc@aol.com
www.crowellhaddenphoto.com

Shelley Heatley Photography
11924 Forest Hill Boulevard
Suite #22-328
Wellington, FL 33414
Phone: (561) 309-8534
E-mail: shelleyheatley@aol.com

Bob Langrish
The Court House
High Street, Bisley
Gloucestershire
GL6 7AA UK
Phone: (44) 014-52770140
Fax: (44) 014-52770146
E-mail: Bob@boblangrish.co.uk
Bob@boblangrish.co.uk

Miranda Lorraine Photography
Contact: Mandy Lorraine
Phone: (717) 529-6247
Cell: (484) 678-1893
E-mail: mirandaslr@msn.com

Charles Mann Photography
9236 Riggs Road
Adelphi, MD
20783-1505
Phone: (301) 434-8094
Fax: (301) 455-4394
E-mail: Charlie@cmannphoto.com

Randi Muster Photography
Mustphoto, Inc
P.O. Box 211323
West Palm Beach, FL 33421
Cell: (314) 591-3800
E-mail: Randi@mustphoto.com

Randy Myers
2141 Marquesas Lane
Lexington, KY 40509
Phone: (859) 299-2223

O'Neill's Photo
Vern O'Neill
1610 South 31 Street, Suite 102
Temple, TX 76504
E-mail: Gr8jump@aol.com

James Parker
Represented by Susan Benson
Somerset Sport Art
P.O. Box 29
Peapack, NJ 07977
Phone: (908) 766-3171
Cell: (908) 313-4744
E-mail: benphoto@benphoto.com

Pennington Galleries
Phyllis Pennington
3700 Woodlawn Drive
Nashville, TN 37215
Phone: (615) 255-3401
E-mail: PTPenn@aol.com
www.PenningtonGalleries.com

Tish Quirk Photography
21 Greenview
Carlsbad, CA 92009
Phone: (760) 431-2772
Cell: (760) 207-4887
E-mail: HorsesUSA@aol.com

Linda Wirtz
P.O. Box 1331
Loxahatchee, FL 33470
Cell: (561) 236-3267
E-mail: lwirtz@bellsouth.net

Robin Wyman
9209 Bellfall Court
Columbia, MD 21045
Phone: (410) 730-6360
E-mail: rwyman7@comcast.net

EQUINE ARTISTS
Barbara Frake Fine Art
Currierville Road
Newton, NJ 03858
Phone: (603) 382-9083
E-mail: Barbara@frakefineart.com
www.FrakeFineArt.com

EQUINE PUBLICATIONS

The Chronicle of the Horse
Robert Banner, Publisher
P.O. Box 46
Middleburg, VA 20118
Phone: (540) 687-6341
www.chronofhorse.com

Horse International
Subscriptions:
*31 40-844-7681
E-mail: subscrip@bcm.nl

Practical Horseman
Sandy Oliynyk, Editor
656 Quince Orchard Road
Carthersburg, MD 20878
Phone: (301) 977-3900
EquiSearch.com
Susan Harding, PRIMEDIA

Sidelines Magazine
Samantha Charles, Publisher
4748 125 Avenue South
Wellington, FL 33467
Phone: (561) 790-6506 or
(561) 818-4502
www.sidelinesnews.com

Stadium Jumping, Inc.
Eugene R. Mische, President
14440 Pierson Road
Wellington, FL 33414
Phone: 800-237-8924
www.stadiumjumping.com

State Line Tack Catalog
www.statelinetack.com

Wellington Lifestyles
Bill Morosco, Publisher
13833 Wellington Trace, #211
Wellington, FL 33414
Phone: (561) 793-7632
E-mail: wellmag@bellsouth.net

COMPUTER IMAGING

Seblin Inc.
www.seblin.com